STATE ARCHIVES OF ASSYRIA STUDIES

VOLUME IX

STATE ARCHIVES OF ASSYRIA STUDIES

Published by the Neo-Assyrian Text Corpus Project
of the University of Helsinki
in co-operation with
the Finnish Oriental Society

Project Director
Simo Parpola

Managing Editor
Robert M. Whiting

VOLUME IX

Sarah C. Melville

THE ROLE OF NAQIA/ZAKUTU IN SARGONID POLITICS

THE NEO-ASSYRIAN TEXT CORPUS PROJECT

State Archives of Assyria Studies is a series of monographic studies relating to and supplementing the text editions published in the SAA series. Manuscripts are accepted in English, French and German. The responsibility for the contents of the volumes rests entirely with the authors.

Set in Times
Typography and layout by Teemu Lipasti
The Assyrian Royal Seal emblem drawn by Dominique Collon from original
Seventh Century B.C. impressions (BM 84672 and 84677) in the British Museum
Ventura Publisher format and custom fonts by Robert M. Whiting and Timo Kiippa
Electronic pasteup by Robert M. Whiting

Printed in Finland
by Vammalan Kirjapaino Oy

ISBN 951-45-9040-6 (Volume 9)
ISSN 1235-1032 (Series)

THE ROLE OF NAQIA/ZAKUTU IN SARGONID POLITICS

By

Sarah C. Melville

THE NEO-ASSYRIAN TEXT CORPUS PROJECT

1999

To the memory of my parents,

Mary Cameron Chamberlin

and

Arthur Newell Chamberlin, III

ACKNOWLEDGEMENTS

This book is a revised and updated version of my dissertation which was finished in 1994 at Yale University. I am grateful to many people who, through their support over the years, have made it possible to complete this project. I owe much to Professors William W. Hallo, Benjamin R. Foster and Gary Beckman whose various approaches to the study of history and historiography have helped me form my own. I am especially indebted to my advisor William Hallo, not only for the patience and guidance which he offered me as a student, but also for his continued interest in this project. Without his encouragement I would have discontinued my research long ago. To Benjamin Foster who has given me much valuable advice, criticized my translations and been a truly inspiring teacher, I owe a huge debt of gratitude. Colleagues Doug Green and Richard Whitekettle gave me much-needed advice about West Semitic names, and I greatly appreciate their time and effort. I would also like to express my thanks to Professor Asger Aaboe whose humor, vast knowledge and perspective allowed this student to see the beauty in difficult and often frustrating work.

Professor Simo Parpola of The University of Helsinki, Director of the Neo-Assyrian Text Corpus Project (State Archives of Assyria), originally suggested the topic of this study and has generously allowed me access to the text corpus, thus enabling me to study recently collated material that would otherwise not have been available to me. Without his encouragement and support this project would have been impossible. I also give sincere thanks to Robert Whiting for his meticulous attention to detail in editing this volume. He has provided many references, suggestions and corrections that have contributed greatly to the finished product, although, of course, any remaining errors are entirely my own responsibility.

I owe many thanks to Ulla Kasten and students in the Babylonian Collection at Yale University for their long-distance help. They answered my many reference questions with speed and accuracy and provided secondary sources that were not otherwise available to me. Ulla is an unfailing friend to whom I am much indebted. I wish to express my sincere gratitude to the Interlibrary Loan Department at St. Lawrence University, particularly Julia Courtney, Laurie Davis and Melissa Jadlos, who worked so hard to provide me with often obscure sources. I could not have written this without their help.

I express my appreciation to the British Museum, London, the Iraq Museum, Baghdad, the Musée du Louvre, Paris, and the Vorderasiatisches Museum, Berlin, for permission to illustrate objects in their collections.

This project is older than my children, James, Christopher, and Timothy and I owe a special debt to them and to their father, Duncan, for cheerfully pitching in to reduce household chaos so that I could complete it. I can never repay my husband for the time and support he has given my work at the expense of his own. He provided constant motivation, perceptive assessment of my arguments, valuable editorial skills, love and a laser printer, and for these things I will always be grateful.

September 1999 Sarah Chamberlin Melville

CONTENTS

CONVENTIONS

Proper names. The names of Neo-Assyrian kings are generally known in their English forms and we follow this convention thus, Sennacherib, Esarhaddon and Ashurbanipal. The subject of this study appears in the sources both with her West Semitic name Naqia and its Akkadian translation, Zakutu. However, for the sake of consistency and to avoid confusion, we refer to her as Naqia. For the spelling of other proper names I follow Simo Parpola and the Neo-Assyrian Text Corpus Project, thus, Ištar-šumu-ereš is corrected to show the expected Assyrian pronunciation Issar-šumu-ereš and Aššur-šarrat is updated to read Libbali-šarrat. Reflecting the erosion of case endings in Assyrian under the influence of Aramaic, many of the names are no longer grammatically correct sentences: Adad-šumu-uṣur rather than Adad-šuma-uṣur, for example.

Geographical names. These follow Parpola, *Neo-Assyrian Toponyms*. AOAT 6 (1970) except where an accepted convention (Babylon, Euphrates, Nineveh, ...) already exists.

Dates. All dates are BC unless otherwise noted.

Transliterations and Translations. Most of the texts quoted in this volume have recently appeared in newly-collated transliteration in the *State Archives of Assyria* series, and this is reflected in the text references. Thus, for example, *SAA* X text numbers replace those of *LAS*; *SAA* VIII text numbers replace those of R.C. Thompson, *The Reports of Magicians and Astrologers of Nineveh and Babylon*, vols. I-II (London, 1900), and so on. In instances where there might be confusion, I give both *SAA* X and *LAS* numbers. A few texts such as Naqia's building inscription and some short votive inscriptions have not appeared in *SAA* and, except for minor alterations, the original transliterations still stand. Professor Simo Parpola, Director of the Neo-Assyrian Text Corpus Project, generously allowed me to use unpublished transliterations of some texts. These are noted as they appear. The translations are my own unless otherwise noted.

ABBREVIATIONS

ABL	Harper, R.F. *Assyrian and Babylonian Letters*. 14 volumes. London and Chicago, 1892-1914
ADD	Johns, C.H.W. *Assyrian Deeds and Documents*. 4 volumes. Cambridge, 1898, 1901, 1901 and 1923
AfO	*Archiv für Orientforschung*
AJSL	*American Journal of Semitic Languages and Literatures*
AOAT	*Alter Orient und Altes Testament*
AOB	*Acta Orientalia Belgica*
AOF	*Altorientalische Forschungen*
AOTU	*Altorientalische Texte und Untersuchungen*
ARINH	Fales, F.M., ed. *Assyrian Royal Inscriptions: New Horizons in Literary, Ideological and Historical Analysis*. Rome, 1981
ARRIM	*Annual Review of the Royal Inscriptions Project of Mesopotamia Project*
ARU	Kohler, J. and A. Ungnad, *Assyrische Rechtsurkunden*. Leipzig, 1913
AS	*Assyriological Studies*
BaM	*Baghdader Mitteilungen*
BASOR	*Bulletin of the American Schools of Oriental Research*
BBEA	Landsberger, B. *Brief des Bischofs von Esagila an König Asarhaddon*. Amsterdam, 1965
BiOr	*Bibliotheca Orientalis*
Borger, *Asarh.*	Borger, R. *Die Inschriften Asarhaddons König von Assyrien*. AfO Beiheft 9. Graz, 1956
Börker-Klähn, *ABVF*	Börker-Klähn, J. *Altvorderasiatische Bildstelen und vergleichbare Felsreliefs*. Baghdader Forschungen 4. Mainz, 1982
Brinkman, *Prelude*	Brinkman, J.A. *Prelude to Empire: Babylonian Society and Politics 747-626 B.C.* Philadelphia, 1984
CAD	*The Assyrian Dictionary of the Oriental Institute of the University of Chicago*. Chicago, 1956-
CAH	*Cambridge Ancient History*. 2nd ed. Cambridge, 1970-
CANE	Sasson, J. et al., eds. *Civilizations of the Ancient Near East*. New York, 1995
CMS Bulletin	*The Canadian Society for Mesopotamian Studies Bulletin*
CRRAI	*Compte rendu de la rencontre assyriologique internationale*
CT	*Cuneiform Texts from Babylonian Tablets in the British Museum.*

Frahm, *Sanherib*	Frahm, E. *Einleitung in die Sanherib-Inschriften.* AfO Beiheft 26. Wien, 1997
Frame, *Babylonia*	Frame, G. *Babylonia 689-627 B.C.: A Political History* Istanbul, 1992
Hallo Fest.	Cohen, M., D.C. Snell, D.B. Weisberg, eds. *The Tablet and the Scroll: Near Eastern Studies in Honor of William W. Hallo.* CDL Press, 1993
HHI	Tadmor, H. and M. Weinfeld, eds. *History, Historiography and Interpretation.* Jerusalem, 1986
JAOS	*Journal of the American Oriental Society*
JCS	*Journal of Cuneiform Studies*
JNES	*Journal of Near Eastern Studies*
Klauber, *PRT*	Klauber, E.G. *Politisch-religiöse Texte aus der Sargonidenzeit.* Leipzig, 1913
Knudtzon, *AGS*	Knudtzon, J.A. *Assyrische Gebete an den Sonnengott für Staat und königliches Haus aus der Zeit Asarhaddons und Asurbanipals.* Leipzig, 1893
Kuhrt, *ANE*	Kuhrt, A. *The Ancient Near East c. 3000-330 B.C.* London, 1995
Kwasman, *NALK*	Kwasman, T. *Neo-Assyrian Legal Documents in the Kouyunjik Collection of the British Museum.* Studia Pohl, Series Maior 14. Rome, 1988
LAS	Parpola, S. *Letters from Assyrian Scholars to the Kings Esarhaddon and Assurbanipal.* 2 volumes. AOAT 5/1-2 Kevelaer and Neukirchen-Vluyn, 1970 and 1983
LSS	*Leipziger Semitistische Studien*
Luckenbill, *Sennacherib*	Luckenbill, D. *The Annals of Sennacherib.* Oriental Institute Publications 2. Chicago, 1924
Mallowan, *Nimrud*	Mallowan, M.E.L. *Nimrud and its Remains.* 2 volumes. New York, 1966
MDVAG	*Mitteilungen der Vorderasiatisch- Aegyptischen Gesellschaft*
Menzel, *Tempel*	Menzel, B. *Assyrische Tempel.* Studia Pohl, Series Maior 10. Rome, 1981
Kinnier Wilson *NWL*	J.V. Kinnier Wilson, *The Nimrud Wine Lists: A study of men and administration at the Assyrian capital in the 8th century B.C.* British School of Archaeology in Iraq, 1972
OrNS	*Orientalia. New Series*
PNA	Radner, K. ed. *The Prosopography of the Neo-Assyrian Empire,* Helsinki, 1998-
Parpola, *Murderer*	Parpola, S. "The Murderer of Sennacherib" in *Death in Mesopotamia.* Edited by B. Alster. Mesopotamia 8. Copenhagen, 1980
Porter, *Images*	Porter, B.N. *Images, Power and Politics: Figurative Aspects of Esarhaddon's Babylonian Policy.* Philadelphia, 1993
Postgate, *NARGD*	Postgate, J.N. *Neo-Assyrian Royal Grants and Decrees.* Studia Pohl, Series Maior 1. Rome, 1969
Postgate, *Taxation*	Postgate, J.N. *Taxation and Conscription in the Assyrian Empire.* Studia Pohl, Series Maior 3. Rome, 1974

Power and Propaganda	Larsen, M.T. (ed.) *Power and Propaganda: a Symposium on Ancient Empires.* Mesopotamia 7. Copenhagen, 1979
RA	*Revue d'assyriologie et d'archéologie orientale*
RLA	*Reallexikon der Asyriologie und vorderasiatischen Archäologie.* Leipzig and Berlin, 1928-
SAA	*State Archives of Assyria*
SAAB	*State Archives of Assyria Bulletin*
SAAS	*State Archives of Assyria Studies*
Schiel, *RT*	Schiel, V. "Notes d'épigraphie et d'archéologie assyriennes." *Recueil de travaux relatifs à la philologie et à l'archéologie égyptiennes et assyriennes*20 (1898) 200-210
Streck, *Assurbanipal*	Streck, M. *Assurbanipal und die letzten assyrischen König bis zum Untergang Nineveh's.* VAB 7. Leipzig, 1916
Tadmor AV	Cogan, M. and I. Eph'al, eds. *Ah, Assyria... Studies in Assyrian History and Ancient Near Eastern Historiography Presented to Hayim Tadmor.* Scripta Hierosolymitana 33. Jerusalem, 1991
TCS	*Texts from Cuneiform Sources*
VAB	*Vorderasiatische Bibliothek*
VTE	Wiseman, D.J. "The Vassal Treaties of Esarhaddon." *Iraq* 20 (1958) 1-100
Waterman, *RCAE*	Waterman, L. *Royal Correspondence of the Assyrian Empire.* 4 volumes. Ann Arbor, 1930-36
WVDOG	*Wissenschaftliche Veröffentlichungen der Deutschen Orient-Gesellschaft*
WO	*Die Welt des Orients*
ZA	*Zeitschrift für Assyriologie*
Zadok, *West Semites*	Zadok, R. *On West Semites in Babylonia during the Chaldean and Achaemenian Periods: An Onomastic Study.* Jerusalem, 1977

ILLUSTRATIONS

INTRODUCTION

Over the past three decades the study of Assyrian civilization, especially of the Neo-Assyrian period, has experienced a renaissance. Excavations at Nimrud and Nineveh have produced extraordinary finds, many of which remain to be fully published. A great deal of new textual material has become accessible, thanks in large part to the efforts of the Neo-Assyrian Text Corpus Project of the University of Helsinki and to the Royal Inscriptions of Mesopotamia Project at the University of Toronto. Much of what had been previously published has been updated, collated and republished. As a result, the body of Neo-Assyrian texts available for study in cuneiform copy, transliteration and/or translation is larger than ever and growing steadily.

In general, however, scholarly energy has been so focused on the publication of new texts and the collation and republication of previously edited texts (and rightly so), that many of them have not yet been subject to historical interpretation.[1] In his commentary volume to *LAS*, Parpola demonstrates what can be accomplished through the intensive study of a coherent group of texts: we now have a refined chronology for the last years of Esarhaddon and the first years of Ashurbanipal, and a fairly comprehensive view of court life during this period. The work of Parpola and other scholars has created many new opportunities for historical inquiry. It is the purpose of this study to evaluate, not just a group of texts that belong together, but all the information, textual, material or otherwise that pertains to the life of the Neo-Assyrian queen, Naqia/Zakutu. In so doing, I hope to clear up some long-standing

[1] Many articles have been written about specific historical problems, but no scholarly monographs devoted solely to the political history of the Sargonid period have appeared. See however the following works which deal with specific aspects of Sargonid political history: P. Gerardi, *Ashurbanipal's Elamite Campaigns: a literary and political study.* (Philadelphia, University of Pennsylvania dissertation, 1987) and B.N. Porter, *Images, Power and Politics: Figurative Aspects of Esarhaddon's Babylonian Policy,* Memoirs of the American Philosophical Society 208 (Philadelphia: American Philosophical Society, 1993) based on her 1987 dissertation. This is in curious contrast to the study of Babylonia during the Neo-Assyrian period. At least three major works have appeared during this time: M. Dietrich, *Die Aramäer Südbabyloniens in der Sargonidenzeit (700-648),* AOAT 7 (Kevalaer and Neukirchen-Vluyn, 1970); J.A. Brinkman, *Prelude to Empire: Babylonian Society and Politics, 747-626 B.C.*, Occasional Publications of the Babylonian Fund 7 (Philadelphia: The University Museum, 1984); G. Frame, *Babylonia 689-627 B.C.: A Political History* (Istanbul: Nederlands Historisch-Archaeologisch Instituut, 1992).

misconceptions about her while shedding further light on the period as a whole.

Our knowledge of the Sargonid period is still far from complete, however, and there has been a tendency among historians to gloss over lacunae with convenient generalizations and assumptions. This has been particularly true in the case of the role played by women in politics. It is common, for example, for modern historians to interpret the structure and power divisions of the Neo-Assyrian royal household based on the assumption that they were analogous to those of the more well-known "harems" of the Ottoman Empire. Thus, we tend to see "harem intrigue" or "female influence" where there is no hard evidence for it.[2] There is, in fact, very little information concerning the "rules" that governed the structure and actions of the king's household ("harem"), royal children or succession practices.[3] As for the personalities that lived there, we know almost nothing beyond the names of a few of them. Because of this it is particularly important that we are always conscious of the preconceptions we bring to our interpretations, and that we are careful to distinguish between fact, speculation and logical conclusion.

The facts of the life of the queen Naqia are few. Her name is West Semitic in origin and of her family we only know that she had a sister, Abi-rami. She was a MÍ.É.GAL of Sennacherib, having entered his harem when he was still crown prince. She bore at least one child, Esarhaddon, and may have had others. We know nothing about her until Esarhaddon was made crown prince in 683.[4] She was at court in Nineveh when her husband was murdered and remained there through the ensuing troubles, during which time she sought news of the future from prophetesses. Most of our information about Naqia dates to the reign of her son, Esarhaddon. To this period belong the letters addressed to her and those in which she is mentioned. We also have the building inscription from a palace that she had built for Esarhaddon, two dedicatory inscriptions, and administrative and economic documents indicating that she was very wealthy and supported a large household staff. When her son died she imposed a loyalty oath on behalf of her grandson, Ashurbanipal, and, although she may have lived longer, that is the last positive evidence we have of her.[5]

This is little enough information on which to base a full-scale study, but the time is ripe to reassess the role of this queen. It has long been recognized that Naqia was an extraordinary personality who may have wielded unprecedented power for a woman. Unfortunately, many assumptions have been made without the benefit of close scrutiny of all the available evidence. In fact, only two articles have been devoted solely to Naqia, and they are now

---

[2] See for example, E. Leichty, "Esarhaddon, King of Assyria" in *CANE,* volume II: 949, and A.K. Grayson, *CAH* III/2: 121.

[3] For a good summary of our knowledge on this topic see Kuhrt, *ANE*: 519-22; 526-29.

[4] For a discussion of this date see below, Chapter II, p. 17, n. 28.

[5] See *SAA* VI, 325 and below, Chapter I, p. 9, n. 15 and Chapter V, p. 86, n. 41, for the possibility that she was alive as late as 663.

badly out of date.[6] Lewy's article is mostly concerned with connecting Naqia with Nitokris of Babylon (a legendary figure in later Greek histories), but she also elaborates on the notion that Naqia ruled Babylonia on behalf of Sennacherib and then Esarhaddon. This theory, which has not been seriously analyzed, has been accepted (up to a point) by some scholars, of whom the most recent and most supportive is Dietrich. Assumptions about Naqia's power and the role she played in her husband's and son's governments have all too frequently been made: she has been credited with the promotion of Esarhaddon to crown prince; a governorship of Babylonia; the reconstruction of Babylon; and the choice of Ashurbanipal as Esarhaddon's heir. Yet no one has systematically evaluated the evidence to see if such allegations will stand.

I propose, in the following study, to analyze and interpret the available sources. Because the primary sources are few, and in many cases, fragmentary or ambiguous, conditional words such as "possible," "probable," "may" and "seems" appear much more often than is desirable. The intention is to present the most reasonable interpretation of the currently available sources. Although I may occasionally allude to different Neo-Assyrian queens or queen mothers, this is not a comparative study. Too little is known about other royal women for us to make useful generalizations about them.

It might seem obvious, for example, to compare Naqia to Semiramis, the illustrious mother of Adad-nirari III, but the story of Semiramis remains so steeped in legend that it is presently impossible to compare the two queens with any degree of accuracy. Many scholars have attempted to distinguish the truth about Semiramis from the legends about her, and, although recent discoveries have added much to our understanding of this woman, we are still far from defining her role in Adad-nirari's government.[7] The time is not yet ripe for a comparative study of these two queens.

Similarly, I do not investigate the question of whether or not the memory of Naqia generated the later legend of Nitokris of Babylon.[8] That subject demands treatment as a facet of the wider problem of the perception of Neo-Assyria in later traditions. The purpose here is to put what we know of Naqia/Zakutu into coherent order, to evaluate it and to determine what Naqia's political role was at the court of three Assyrian kings, Sennacherib, Esarhaddon and Ashurbanipal.

---

[6] B. Meissner, "Naki'a," *MDVAG* 8/3 (1903): 96-101 and H. Lewy, "Nitokris-Naqî'a," *JNES* 11 (1952): 264-86. Note, however, the more recent article by J. Boncquet, "De Koningin-moeder in de Neo-Assyrische periode," AOB 4 (Leuven, 1986): 183-94, which gives a general overview of the evidence conerning Naqia.

[7] See most recently W. Schramm, "War Semiramis assyrische Regentin?" *Historia* 21 (1972): 513ff; G. Pettinato, *Semiramis: Herrin über Assur und Babylon,* (Artemis: Zürich and Munich, 1988); S.S. Ahmad, *Simiramis,* (Azamiyah, Baghdad: Dar al-Shun al-Thagafiyah al-Amnah, 1989); V. Donbaz, "Two Neo-Assyrian Stelae in the Antakya and Kahramanmaraş Museums," *ARRIM* 8 (1990): 5-24; and M. Weinfeld, "Semiramis: Her Name and Origin," *Tadmor AV*: 99-103.

[8] See Lewy, *JNES* 11: 264-86; and Weinfeld, *Tadmor AV*: 102.

I begin by discussing the variety of primary sources to be used, the problems involved in their use, and my methods of dealing with them. In the rest of the book I investigate and interpret the events of Naqia's life with a view to discovering what part she played as queen, queen mother and dowager queen mother; what kind of power she wielded and to what purpose she wielded it. Chapter II deals with Naqia's origins and the question of her rise to prominence as the queen of Sennacherib. Chapters III and IV follow her career as Esarhaddon's queen mother, and Chapter V discusses the culmination of her career when her grandson, Ashurbanipal, became king. This is followed by a brief concluding summary and appendices.

CHAPTER I

SOURCES

In order to reconstruct the life of the Neo-Assyrian queen Naqia we have had to consult a wide variety of sources.[1] These may be divided into two basic groups: sources which directly pertain to the queen (i.e. mention her name or titles) and those which do not concern her specifically but which provide background or supplementary information. We are aided in our study of Naqia/Zakutu by the fact that so many primary sources have been published and many of these have been reworked recently to provide up-to-date transliterations and translations. Because the texts themselves are often difficult to interpret and almost never dated, we are faced with two main problems: dating and attribution. Although the chronology for the period in question (c. 705-650 BC) has been well established and provides us with a clear framework,[2] assigning specific dates to texts or objects is in almost every case problematic. In many instances it is not even possible to attribute a text unequivocally to Naqia. The fact that she was active during three reigns further complicates the issue. In the following I will give a general description of all sources used and discuss some of the problems involved in their use. More detailed evaluations of the texts appear throughout this book. See Appendix A for a catalog of all the sources pertaining to Naqia, with references, museum and text numbers.

Letters

A large letter corpus survives from the archives of the Neo-Assyrian kings. Much of this was published in cuneiform copy by Harper in *ABL* (1892-1914) and edited by Waterman in *RCAE* (1930-1936) and by Pfeiffer in *State Letters*

---

[1] In order to avoid the proliferation of long references, many abbreviations are used in this chapter. For full references consult the list of abbreviations and the bibliography.

[2] The Assyrian eponym canon is preserved through 648 BC. See A. Ungnad, "Eponymen," *RLA* 2: 412-57. For the later eponyms see M. Falkner, "Die Eponymen der spätassyrischen Zeit," *AfO* 17 (1954-56): 100-20. These two works have been superseded for the most part by A.R. Millard, *The Eponyms of the Assyrian Empire, 910-612 BC*. SAAS 2 (1994).

of Assyria (1935). Although these publications made a large body of material available to scholars, they contain many mistakes and misreadings and are now quite out of date. In *LAS*, Parpola presents the correspondence of the court scholars with the kings Esarhaddon and Ashurbanipal, re-editing much of *ABL* and providing a great deal of additional material. Both Parpola in *CT* 53, and Dietrich in *CT* 54, have published cuneiform copies of additional texts and fragments and both scholars are working on the republication of the Harper letters.[3] Recently, in *SAA* X, Parpola has published a reworking of *LAS* with additional material and Cole and Machinist have published further letters in *SAA* XIII. All the letters cited in this paper that appeared in *ABL* will be referred to by *ABL* number unless they have since been edited in *LAS*, *SAA* X, or in *SAA* XIII in which case I cite the newest number. Transliterations of some of the letters quoted in this paper were kindly provided by Simo Parpola of the Neo-Assyrian Text Corpus Project of the University of Helsinki and in many instances improve upon the older editions. I have altered some of these transliterations slightly, for the sake of consistency. All translations are my own unless otherwise noted.

Among the Neo-Assyrian royal correspondence are a number of letters addressed to the queen mother. Five or six letters were addressed to her from Assyrian scholars/officials; four letters were written to her by Babylonian officials; one letter was written to her from the king. In addition, there are thirteen or more[4] letters mentioning the queen mother that were written to the king or crown prince. No letter survives that was written by the queen mother nor is there any relevant correspondence from the time when she was queen.[5]

Letters present a multiplicity of problems for scholars who use them as source material.[6] Because they are private communications, the language in which they are written tends to be idiomatic. Since the context of any given letter was of course understood by both the writer and receiver, most information is stated without explanation: thus particular days may be referred to but months and years left out; people named without identification; or the reverse, mentioned but not named. We are faced with a further problem when we try to distinguish the officials writing the letters. Many of these men bear common names and they usually do not identify their official status. For example, at least three different men named Ašaredu are known to have been active in Babylonia during Esarhaddon's and Ashurbanipal's reigns. One of them wrote a letter to the queen mother. Any interpretation of this letter is partly dependent upon the identification of the official writing it. In attempting to attribute a text to a certain official, we look at the opening greeting

---

[3] Many of the Harper letters have been edited in articles by various scholars, for which see R. Borger, *Handbuch der Keilschriftliteratur,* volumes I and II under Harper.

[4] In one or two cases it is not clear whether the letter refers to the queen mother.

[5] Although see M. Dietrich, "Neue Quellen zur Geschichte Babyloniens, II," *WO* 4 (1967-8): 203, where he suggests that the tiny fragment *CT* 54, 279 is a letter to Sennacherib which may refer to a queen, possibly Naqia.

[6] For a discussion of the problems involved in working with letters see S. Parpola, "Assyrian Royal Inscriptions and Neo-Assyrian Letters," *ARINH*, especially pages 125ff.

formula, content of the letter, other people mentioned, peculiarities of spelling and grammar in comparison to other letters by this author, point of origin and datable references.

Assigning dates to these letters poses another problem, since not one of them is explicitly dated. Because we are only dealing with some nineteen letters (a tiny fraction of the royal correspondence), and because they do not form a coherent group (some are Assyrian, some Babylonian, some deal with religious matters and some medical matters, for instance), we generally do not find connections among them to elucidate their dating.[7] Although astronomical observations in the letters edited by Parpola in *LAS* allowed him to determine specific dates for many of them, astronomical notation does not appear in our letters, and so we must rely on less explicit information: what is known about the career of the author, any datable reference (i.e. to a campaign, particular eclipse or religious festival), reference to other people (e.g., if the letter is written to the crown prince Ashurbanipal we know that it dates between 672 and 669 BC). In many cases I have been able to narrow the date of a letter down to a few years, but I have not suggested specific dates unless the evidence seemed to go well beyond speculation.

Royal Inscriptions

The royal inscriptions of the Neo-Assyrian kings are very useful for reconstruction of historical events[8] and contain some important anecdotal information in spite of the chronological difficulties that some of them pose. Thus, for example, Esarhaddon's annals relate information about Na'id-Marduk's appointment to be governor of the Sealand and may help determine when he left office,[9] which may in turn help us fix a *terminus post quem* and *terminus ante quem* for *ABL* 917, a letter written by Na'id-Marduk to the queen mother, Naqia.

The queen mother herself wrote a building inscription dedicating a palace that she had built at Nineveh for Esarhaddon when he was king. This inscription exists in three fragmentary copies which have been published by Borger.[10]

[7] With the exception of the group of letters (*SAA* X, 200, 201, 244, and 297) that deal with Naqia's illness.

[8] For differing views about the reliability of Neo-Assyrian royal inscriptions see A.K. Grayson, "Histories and Historians of the Ancient Near East: Assyria and Babylonia," *OrNS* 49 (1980): 140-94; M. Cogan, "A Plaidoyer on Behalf of the Royal Scribes," *Tadmor AV*: 121-28.

[9] Borger, *Asarh.*, 47, §27, Nin A, Ep. 4: 63-64 and page 64.

[10] Borger, *Asarh.*, 115-16, §86, and R. Borger, "König Sanheribs Eheglück," *ARRIM* 6 (1988): 7 and 11.

Monumental inscription/relief

Naqia is depicted and identified by name on the fragment of a bronze relief which is now in the Louvre. The relief is inscribed with part of a royal inscription, which has not as yet been positively identified. First published by Parrot and Nougayrol, it has since been discussed by various other scholars.[11]

Dedicatory inscriptions

Naqia made dedicatory offerings on behalf of Esarhaddon and herself and their inscriptions survive on an interesting tablet, one side of which bears the dedication from Zakutu to the goddess Mullissu and the other side of which is inscribed with the dedication of Naqia to the "Lady" of Nineveh (Issar). This tablet was published in cuneiform copy by Johns in *ADD* 645 and in transliteration and translation by Kohler and Ungnad in *ARU* 14.

An inscribed gemstone belonging to Naqia is part of a private collection. Its inscription was published by Scheil[12] and subsequently by Galter.[13] Recently, Van De Mieroop published a similar stone and the necklace to which it belongs.[14] Both objects were probably dedications to gods or goddesses and were worn on the dieties' statues.

Economic and administrative documents

A vast number of economic and administrative documents have survived from the Neo-Assyrian period. Most of these texts were first published in cuneiform copy by Johns in *ADD*, and subsequently edited by Kohler and Ungnad in *ARU*. Recently many of the legal documents have been updated and re-edited by Kwasman in *NALK* and by Kwasman and Parpola in *SAA* VI. Postgate edited a number of the administrative documents in *NARGD* and in *Taxation*. Most recently many of these texts have been reworked by Fales and Postgate in *SAA* VII and by Kataja and Whiting in *SAA* XII. From this point on, economic and administrative documents will be referred to by the number used to identify them in the most recent edition of the text. Thus the number identifying a text in *SAA* VII will supersede the number the text was given in *ADD, ARU* or any other edition.

---

[11] A. Parrot, and J. Nougayrol, "Asarhaddon et Naq'ia sur un bronze du Louvre (AO 20.185)," *Syria* 33 (1956): 147-60. For further references see J. Börker-Klähn, *ABVF*: 220 and 221.

[12] V. Scheil, *RT* 20 (1898): 200. For further references see Lewy, *JNES* 11: 272, n. 41.

[13] D.H. Galter, "On Beads and Curses," *ARRIM* 5 (1987): 22.

[14] M. Van De Mieroop, "An Inscribed Bead of Queen Zakûtu," in *Hallo Fest.*: 259-60.

Many of the legal documents are dated, but the majority have had the date broken away or, more rarely, were never dated. Most of our information concerning the size, structure, and economic base of the households of the queen and queen mother comes from these texts. In the witness lists and the principals named in them we can identify the officials that made up these households. Court administrative documents help to give us a picture of the position that the queen and queen mother held at court, how much in terms of food and goods they received from the king and what, if anything, they were expected to pay in taxes. These documents are full of vital information yet there are many problems involved in their use. For instance, the fact that in economic and administrative texts, members of the royal family were usually referred to by title, rather than name, or name plus title, can make it extremely difficult to be certain of the identity of the person involved if the text is not dated. Thus, if an economic document refers to an official of the queen mother, unless the date is preserved, we can only assign it to Naqia if the prosopographical information allows. We encounter similar difficulties in texts which refer to a queen and are dated *after* the death of Aššur-nadin-šumi (c. 694 BC) but *before* the probable date of Esarhaddon's appointment as crown prince (c. 683 BC). In this case we are left with the question, did the mother of Aššur-nadin-šumi remain first wife until a second crown prince was appointed or did Naqia gain power before Esarhaddon's appointment, and if so, when? *SAA* VI, 325 presents a further problem: the text dates to 663 and line 2 apparently refers to the scribe of the queen mother.[15] But if Ešarra-ḫamat, who died in 672, was Ashurbanipal's mother this text can only refer to Naqia. Otherwise we must assume that Ashurbanipal's mother lived into his reign.[16] We must also decide whether, in any given transaction where an official is identified as the officer of the queen or queen mother, he is acting on his own behalf or on behalf of his superior. All of these questions will be addressed in some detail in this work.

Adê *agreements*

The *adê* agreements from the Neo-Assyrian period have most recently been treated by Parpola,[17] and by Parpola and Watanabe in *SAA* II. Five treaties are of particular interest to us here: the succession treaty of Sennacherib (*SAA* II, 3) in which a loyalty oath is exacted on behalf of the crown prince (Esarhaddon?), the accession treaty of Esarhaddon (*SAA* II, 4), the succession treaty of 672 (*SAA* II, 6), the loyalty oath of 670 (*SAA* II, 7) and the Zakutu

[15] The line is partly restored: A.BA ⌜*ša* AMA!⌝.[MAN].

[16] As do M. Streck, *Assurbanipal*: 392-95 and A.K. Grayson, *CAH* III/2: 139.

[17] S. Parpola, "Neo-Assyrian Treaties from the Royal Archives of Nineveh," *JCS* 39 (1987): 161-89.

treaty (*SAA* II, 8) in which the queen mother exacts a loyalty oath on behalf of her grandson, Ashurbanipal.

Queries

A very large body of tablets including queries to the god Šamaš and extispicy reports were first edited by Knudtzon in *AGS* (1893) and Klauber in *PRT* (1913). The whole corpus, with additions, has recently been re-edited by Starr in *SAA* IV.

Two groups of these queries are of interest to us here: appointment queries in which Esarhaddon asks whether a specific individual will be loyal if appointed to a certain post; and medical queries in which the gods are asked whether an individual will recover from an illness. *SAA* IV, 151 belongs to the former group and is a query regarding the appointment of an unnamed individual to the household guard of Naqia. *SAA* IV, 190 (and possibly 191) is a medical query which asks whether Naqia will recover from an illness, said to have been caused "by the hand of the god Iqbi-damiq."

Oracles

A number of oracular statements have survived concerning the accession of Esarhaddon. Two of these (K4310 and K12033 + 82-5-22,527) are addressed to the king and the queen mother and at least one (K6259) is addressed to the queen mother alone. These were first published by Pinches ($4R^2$, 61) and Langdon (*TI* Taf. IIf) and have been more recently studied in a number of papers by several different scholars, most notably Weippert, Ellis and Fales/Lanfranchi.[18] Simo Parpola has now re-edited the entire Neo-Assyrian oracular corpus with an important commentary in *SAA* IX.[19]

---

[18] M. Weippert, "Assyrische Prophetien der Zeit Asarhaddons und Assurbanipals," *ARINH*: 94ff, M. deJong Ellis, "Observations on Mesopotamian Oracles and Prophetic Texts: Literary and Historiographic Considerations," *JCS* 41 (1989):127-86, and F.M. Fales and G.B. Lanfranchi, "The Impact of Oracular Material on the Political Utterances and Political Action of the Sargonid Dynasty," in J.-G. Heintz (ed.), *Oracles et propheties dans l'antiquité* (Travaux du Centre de Recherche sur le Proche-Orient et la Grèce Antiques 15, Paris 1997): 99-114. See also the extensive bibliography given by Parpola in *SAA* IX: cix-cxii.

[19] See also the contribution to the study of Assyrian oracles by Martti Nissinen, *References to Prophecy in Neo-Assyrian Sources*. SAAS 7 (1998).

Miscellaneous

There are several seal impressions that were published by Reade[20] which are similar to the bronze relief of Naqia in that they show a woman standing behind the king performing an act of worship. In addition it is possible that one of the standing stones from Assur bears the name of one of Sennacherib's wives, and sometimes it has been attributed to Naqia, although the piece is so damaged that any identification is doubtful.[21]

---

[20] J.E. Reade, "Was Sennacherib a Feminist?" *CRRAI* 33 (1986): 139-45.

[21] W. Andrae, *Die Stelenreihen in Assur*, WVDOG 24 (Leipzig, 1913): no. 4 and see also Frahm, *Sanherib*: 184-85.

CHAPTER II

ANTECEDENTS TO POWER: NAQIA AS MÍ.É.GAL

At some point during the reign of Sargon II (721-705) Naqia joined the household of the Crown Prince Sennacherib. Based on the estimated chronology for other members of the family, it is most likely that Naqia bore her son, Esarhaddon, between 713 and 711. Thus Naqia must have entered Sennacherib's household by at least c. 713.[1] Various scholars have speculated about Naqia's origins, although there is no certain evidence.

The name Naqia is West Semitic, apparently a *qattil* pattern based on the root NQ' ("pure"),[2] with the feminine ending *ā*: Naqqi'ā.[3] In contemporary sources there are other examples of names based on this root, but they do not elucidate the question of origin.[4] By the end of the 8th century, West Semitic names were becoming more and more common in Assyria and

---

[1] Any date outside this range does not coordinate with what we know of the other members of his family. For example, Aššur-nadin-šumi, the eldest of Sennacherib's sons, was made ruler of Babylonia in 699 (Luckenbill, *Sennacherib* p. 35, ll. 71-74), so he must have been approximately eighteen at the time. Even considering that some of Sennacherib's children could have been born in the same year to different mothers, we can assume that there must have been a gap of at least five years between Aššur-nadin-šumi and Esarhaddon, who, by his own admission was the youngest of the king's sons (Borger, *Asarh.* 40, §27, Nin A and F, Ep. 2: 8-14). This would put Esarhaddon's birth at circa 713, which in turn would allow Ashurbanipal, also the youngest son, to be just eighteen when Esarhaddon died. See Parpola *LAS* 2: n. 390. Contrary to Leichty, *CANE*: 949, who asserts that "Esarhaddon was born when Naqia was already well into her thirties ...," there is no evidence whatsoever suggesting Naqia's age. Leichty's statement is based on the assumption that Naqia was Sennacherib's only queen and had somehow maintained her position in spite of being childless as other sons were born to different mothers. Although this is technically possible, it is extremely unlikely. See below, pp. 20-22 for a discussion of Naqia's position with relation to Sennacherib's other wives.

[2] Zadok, *West Semites*: 135.

[3] Naqia is spelled without the doubling of the second consonant that occurs in the *qattil*, which may suggest that it is formed on the *qatil* base. Zadok defines it as an example of the *qattil* (*West Semites*: 135 and 171) and it is possible that the lack of doubling may be attributed to the vagaries of Akkadian orthography.

[4] For example, the masculine name *Na-qí-iá* (*ABL* 906, obv. 8); and Aramaic Naqqay (Zadok, *West Semites*: 135).

Babylonia;[5] thus the fact that a name is West Semitic cannot be used to determine the bearer's point of origin.[6] Naqia's name alone cannot tell us where she came from, nor does it indicate that she was born outside of Assyria proper.[7]

Because Naqia sometimes adopted the Akkadian name Zakutu, a translation of Naqia, scholars have assumed that she was not native to Assyria. Thus Johns[8] and Waterman[9] suggest that Naqia was Hebrew[10] and the latter contends that she was one of the women that Hezekiah sent to Sennacherib in 701. Although linguistically speaking it is possible that Naqia was Hebrew, she cannot have joined the harem at such a late date, since this would have delayed Esarhaddon's birth so long that Ashurbanipal would have been impossibly young at the time of his father's death.[11] The recent discovery of the grave of Atalia, one of Sargon II's wives,[12] does suggest a Hebrew connection at the right time,[13] but this may not have any bearing on the question of Naqia's origins.

Other scholars connect Naqia to the Aramaean tribes living in Babylonia, rather than to those of Syria and the west.[14] Four letters were written to Naqia

---

5 See Zadok, *West Semites*, passim; F.M. Fales, "A List of Assyrian and West Semitic Women's Names," *Iraq* 41 (1979): 55-73; and F.M. Fales, "On Aramaic Onomastics in the Neo-Assyrian Period," *Oriens Antiquus* 16 (1977): 41-68.

6 Note Millard's comment, "Perhaps by the seventh century B.C. there was no racial distinction, only a difference of language. There is some risk in attributing nationality on the basis of personal names." A.R. Millard, "Assyrians and Arameans," *Iraq* 45 (1983): 104.

7 The names of at least two of the "queens," Iabaia and Atalia, from the recently discovered royal tombs at Nimrud are also West Semitic, but this does not necessarily mean that they were foreign. For the possibility that Atalia is a Hebrew name see below. For information about the graves and their occupants see A. Harrak, "The Royal Tombs of Nimrud and Their Jewelry," *CMS Bulletin* 20 (1990): 5-14 and A. Fadhil, "Die in Nimrud/Kalḫu aufgefundene Grabinschrift der Jabâ," *BaM* 21 (1990): 461-70; A. George, "Royal Tombs at Nimrud," *Minerva* I/1 (1990) 29-31.

8 Johns, *ADD* IV: 160.

9 Waterman, *RCAE* III: 327.

10 Weinfeld, *Tadmor AV*: 102, comments that "Naqi'a/Zakutu, Sennacherib's wife, was of Syrian or even Hebrew origin." He cites as his source a dissertation (in Hebrew and unavailable to me) by S. Arbeli, *Women in the Bible in Position of Privilege and Their Involvement in Social and Political Affairs: A Comparative Study using Ancient Near Eastern Sources,* Dissertation (Jerusalem: Hebrew University, 1984): 73ff.

11 If Esarhaddon had been born in 700, he would have been not quite twenty when his father was murdered, which would mean that Ashurbanipal could not have been much over puberty (c. 12) when Esarhaddon died; this we know was not the case. Ashurbanipal was of age in 669 and already had at least one child. For further remarks about the birthdates of the Sargonid kings see Parpola, *LAS* II: 231, n. 390.

12 See above note 7.

13 The royal name Atalia is attested in the Bible (2 Kings 8:26; 11:1-3, 13-14 and 20; 1 Chronicles 8:26; 2 Chronicles: 22:2, 10-12; 23:12-13, and 21; 24:7; Ezra: 8:7).

14 See for example, Lewy, *JNES* 11: 272 n.42 in which she writes: "We need not, therefore, hesitate to define ^{f}*Na-qi-ʾ-a* as an adequate Assyrian rendering of an old

from Babylonia during Esarhaddon's reign[15] and some scholars, in particular Schmidtke and Winckler, have taken these as indications both that Naqia came from the area and that she governed it.[16] However, the contents of these letters, which will be discussed in detail in subsequent chapters, give us no information as to Naqia's origins, and reveal little about her involvement in the government of the area. Taking a different tack, Lewy argues that Naqia must have been brought to Assyria by Sargon II in 712, after he campaigned in northern Babylonia and took the area around and including Lahiru. Her argument is based on the fact that Naqia later had an estate in Lahiru,[17] but it should be pointed out that other members of the royal family held land there also,[18] so this can hardly be seen as an indication that she came from the area.

According to Nougayrol, Naqia was probably born in Babylonia but her family may have originated in the Harran area.[19] The suggestion that Naqia orignially came from the West is based on artistic evidence. On the fragment of a bronze relief now in the Louvre (AO 20.185), Naqia is depicted standing behind the king. She holds a mirror in her left hand and some sort of plant in her right hand. In their discussion of this piece, Parrot and Nougayrol point out that the motif of a woman holding a mirror is Syrian/Anatolian in origin and appears in Assyrian art here for the first time.[20] Given the Assyrian sculptors' dedication to accurate renderings of costume and accoutrements, it is likely that Naqia actually held a mirror during the performance of some religious rite(s), but the mirror, far from being a personal emblem introduced by Naqia, must be intimately tied to the Assyrian notion of queenship. It may represent the queen as earthly representative of Aššur's consort.[21]

The only other piece of information we have about Naqia is that she had a sister, Abi-rami (also a West Semitic name[22]) who purchased the use of some

dialectal form used by the Aramaeans of Southern Babylonia in the sense of the Biblical Aramaic **naqi̯ā, 'Pura.'*"

15 The letters are *ABL* 254 and 917 and *SAA* X, 154 and 313. For a full discussion of these letters and their dating see below Chapters III and IV.

16 F. Schmidtke, *Asarhaddons Statthalterschaft in Babylonien und seine Thronbesteigung in Assyrien 681 v. Chr.*, AOTU 1/2 (Leiden, 1916): 124-30 and H. Winckler, *AOF* II (Leipzig, 1898): 189.

17 Lewy, *JNES* 11 (1957): 273-74 referring to *ADD* 301 (= *SAA* VI, 255).

18 Šamaš-šumu-ukin apparently resided at Lahiru when he was crown prince (Parpola, *LAS* II: 271) and the queen (Libbali-šarrat) owned property there in 668 (Kwasman, *NALK* 174).

19 Parrot and Nougayrol, *Syria* 33: 158.

20 Parrot and Nougayrol, *Syria* 33: 139, n. 3, and 158.

21 See Reade, *CRRAI* 33 (1986): 143, and S. Parpola *Assyrian Prophecies*, *SAA* IX (1997): xviii-xxv and xcviii n. 159, where Parpola notes that the mirror is an attribute of the goddess Mullissu. Very little is known about the role of royal women in the state cult, however. See B. Menzel, *Assyrische Tempel*. 2 vols. Studia Pohl, Series Maior 10. (Rome: Biblical Institue Press, 1981).

22 Borger, *ARRIM* 6: 7. See now PNA 1/I: 14.

land in the vicinity of Baruri in 674.[23] Abi-rami is not known from any other source, and the location of the village Baruri has not been identified. We can only guess at the position she may have held, but the economic document does indicate that she had sufficient status to act on her own behalf.

Although it is tempting to assume that Naqia adopted the name Zakutu because she was a foreigner and wished to appear Assyrian, it must be remembered that Zakutu, being a simple translation of Naqia, is artificial as a name and therefore would not have seemed especially Assyrian. In any case there is no reason to believe that having a West Semitic name would have been seen as unusual or particularly foreign. One must also exercise caution when assigning some significance to Naqia's bilingual name use because only six texts survive that include her names.[24] The name Naqia appears in four extant texts, three of which date securely to Esarhaddon's reign.[25] The name Zakutu is known from only three texts,[26] which date to Esarhaddon's reign or later. At present there is no satisfactory way to resolve the problem of Naqia's origin. It is certainly possible that she came from outside Assyria proper, but lacking further evidence, it is not safe simply to assume that she did so.[27]

Naqia as Sennacherib's queen

The promotion of Esarhaddon to the position of Crown Prince has long intrigued Assyriologists, especially since it apparently led to the murder of Sennacherib by one of his other sons. It has generally been assumed that Esarhaddon achieved this position because of the influence his powerful mother had over Sennacherib. Consideration of all the available evidence,

---

[23] T. Kwasman and S. Parpola, *Legal Transactions of the Royal Court at Nineveh,* SAA VI (1981): 252. The date of the text is 674, eponymy of Šarru-nuri. See also S. Herbordt, *Neuassyrische Glyptik des 8.-7. Jh. v. Chr. unter besonderer Berücksichtigung der Siegelungen auf Tafeln und Tonverschlüssen.* SAAS I (1992): 208 and Taf. 18,27. The text is from Nineveh and the seal owner from Hazzat (modern Gaza).

[24] The possible religious or political significance of the use of two names is discussed in Chapter III.

[25] Parrot and Nougayrol, *Syria* 33; Kohler and Ungnad, *ARU* 14; I. Starr, *Queries to the Sungod. SAA* IV (1990): 151 and V. Scheil, *RT* 20 (1898): 200, no. 8. Note that it is not possible to ascertain from Scheil whether or not the inscription is broken after Sennacherib's name or ended with it and therefore it cannot be dated to one reign in particular.

[26] *ARU* 14 and S. Parpola and K. Watanabe, *Neo-Assyrian Treaties and Loyalty Oaths. SAA* II (1988) and the necklace published by Van De Mieroop, *Hallo Fest.*: 259-61.

[27] See also the brief discussion and additional bibliography in Bob Becking, *The Fall of Samaria: An Historical and Archaelological Study,* Studies in the History of the Ancient Near East 2 (Leiden: E.J. Brill, 1992), 91-92.

however, makes it clear that Esarhaddon's promotion in 683[28] was the culmination of a concatenation of events that started in 694[29] with the death of the crown prince, Aššur-nadin-šumi. Unfortunately, the sequence of these events is anything but clear and is certainly open to interpretation. In order to follow Naqia's rise to power and decide just how great her influence was, it is vital to determine what happened during the interval between 694 and 683. That is, we must ascertain the status of Sennacherib's wives and sons during this period: who was queen? who, if anyone, was crown prince? If we can answer these questions we will have a much clearer perception of Naqia's position in Sennacherib's harem.

Very little is known about Sennacherib's harem beyond the names of seven of his children:[30] six boys – Aššur-nadin-šumi, Urad-Mullissu, Aššur-šumu-ušabši, Aššur-ili-muballissu, Esarhaddon, and perhaps Nergal-šumu-[ibni][31] – and one daughter, Šadditu. With the obvious exception of Naqia and Esarhaddon, we cannot say who the mothers of these children were, although Naqia was certainly *not* the mother of Aššur-nadin-šumi or Urad-Mullissu.[32] It does,

---

[28] See Parpola and Watanabe, *SAA* II: xxviii, and S. Parpola, "Neo-Assyrian Treaties from the Royal Archives of Nineveh," *JCS* 39 (1987): 164 and 180, for full discussions of Sennacherib's succession treaty which Parpola dates to 683 or 682 on the basis of the god list. He further suggests that it may have been enacted in Nisan during the New Year's Festival at the *Bīt Akītu* in Assur. Recently, Kwasman and Parpola, *SAA* VI: xxxiv rule out 682 as a possible date for Esarhaddon's appointment and call Nisan 683 "the most likely time of the appointment." There are two undated Sennacherib texts which have been taken by some scholars to indicate an earlier date for Esarhaddon's promotion. *ABL* 1452 (see now L. Kataja and R. Whiting, *Grants, Decrees and Gifts of the Neo-Assyrian Period. SAA* XII, 88) is a gift of jewelry (spoil from Bit-Amukanni) from Sennacherib to Esarhaddon. The text also states that Esarhaddon's name shall be changed to Aššur-etel-lu-mukin-apli ("Aššur, prince of the gods, is establishing an heir"), which suggests that the gift was made at the time of his promotion. Sennacherib did not campaign in Babylonia after the fall of Babylon in 689, but the mention of booty from Bit-Amukanni need not indicate that the gift was made immediately after one of Sennacherib's Babylonian campaigns. The other text, Luckenbill, *Sennacherib*: 22, from Assur, is a dedication of the building of a shrine to Aššur, "for the life of my youngest son ..." However, the fact that Esarhaddon is not given the title "*mār šarri rabû ša bēt rēdûti*," which was expressly invented for him, indicates that he had not yet attained the position of Crown Prince.

[29] Aššur-nadin-šumi was captured in 694. But see now I.L. Finkel, "A Report on Extispicies Performed for Sennacherib on Account of His Son Aššur-nadin-šumi," *SAAB* 1 (1987): 53, which refers to a (long lost) cuneiform text relating Sennacherib's inquiry to a god about the fate of his crown prince. This brings up an important point. Although Aššur-nadin-šumi disappeared in 694 we do not know exactly when he died. It is certainly possible that Sennacherib made efforts to recover the lost prince. In any case, Sennacherib would not have appointed another crown prince until he was certain the first one was not coming back. However, it seems safe to assume that Aššur-nadin-šumi's death occured before or during Sennacherib's next Babylonian campaign.

[30] Most of them are named in K6109 (Bezold, *Cat*. II: 763; "a list of gods and persons"). See also Borger, *ARRIM* 6 (1988): 8 and Frahm, *Sanherib*: 3-4.

[31] Borger, *ARRIM* 6: 8, and also Kwasman and Parpola, *SAA* VI: xxxiii.

[32] Parpola, *Murderer*: 175.

however, seem likely that she was the mother of Šadditu.[33] Aššur-nadin-šumi was the eldest son and Esarhaddon the youngest, but we cannot determine the order of the other children with assurance, although it is probable that Urad-Mullissu was the second oldest brother.[34] We must remember, however, that aside from Aššur-nadin-šumi and his mother, we have no way of knowing how the other women of the household and their sons were ranked.

We know the name of one of Sennacherib's wives, Tašmetum-šarrat, from an unusual text inscribed on a doorway in Sennacherib's palace at Nineveh.[35] In view of the fact that this woman is described in the text as the "MÍ.É.GAL *ḫīrtu narāmtia*" (the queen, my beloved wife) it is possible that she was his first queen, the mother of Aššur-nadin-šumi.[36] Certainly this woman held an exalted position at some point during Sennacherib's reign and if she was *not* the mother of Sennacherib's eldest son, then Tašmetum-šarrat was probably first wife after Aššur-nadin-šumi's mother but before Naqia, which fits the chronology of Sennacherib's palace, built between roughly 703 and 693.[37] According to Borger, the bull inscriptions were probably written after 694, therefore after the death of the crown prince.[38] It is possible that Tašmetum-šarrat was simply a young (politically insignificant) girl in Sennacherib's harem who happened to catch the fancy of the aging monarch and was never first queen at all,[39] but given the length and eloquence of the inscription dedicating palace rooms to her, this seems less likely.

In addition, the name of what might have been one of Sennacherib's wives was removed, apparently intentionally, from the inscription on one of the standing stones at Assur.[40] The inscription is so badly damaged that it is impossible to tell what the name might have been or even if it really belonged to a wife of the king. Andrae restored ^{f}SU-[*x x x*] GAL(?)-*a* in line 2,[41] but

---

[33] Given the fact that she is the only known sister of Esarhaddon and is known to have been considered part of the royal family as late as 672 (see *SAA* X, 273 in which Nabû-nadin-šumi performs a ritual on her behalf) it seems likely that they were more than half-siblings.

[34] Parpola, *Murderer*: n. 31.

[35] H. Galter, L. Levine, and J. Reade, "The Colossi of Sennacherib's Palace and their Inscriptions," *ARRIM* 4 (1986): 32; and Borger, *ARRIM* 6: 5-11. Tašmetum-šarrat is also known from a vase inscription: Luckenbill, *Sennacherib*: I 28. See now Frahm, *Sanherib*: 121 and 184.

[36] J.E. Reade, "Was Sennacherib a Feminist?" *CRRAI* 33 (1986): 141, suggests that Tašmetum-šarrat might be the mother of Aššur-nadin-šumi. In this short inscription she receives more attention than any other woman at Sennacherib's court.

[37] J.M. Russell, *Sennacherib's Palace without Rival at Nineveh* (Chicago: University of Chicago Press, 1991): 88-93.

[38] Borger, *ARRIM* 6: 6.

[39] Borger, *ARRIM* 6: 6.

[40] W. Andrae, *Die Stelenreihen in Assur*, WVDOG 24 (Leipzig, 1913): 9. Frahm, *Sanherib*: 185, makes the interesting suggestion that the name was removed by Naqia or Esarhaddon after Sennacherib's murder.

[41] W. Andrae, *Die Stelenreihen in Assur*, WVDOG 24 (Leipzig, 1913): 10 (no. 4).

Grayson considers it possible the the stela be attributed to Naqia, although he does not explain why.[42] If this stone does belong to another one of Sennacherib's wives then we must consider the possibility of a third queen, for the fact that she had enough status to erect a stone at Assur probably indicates that she was first wife at some point.

Of course our interpretation of the evidence is partly dependent on our acceptance or rejection of certain assumptions about the Assyrian harem and succession practices.[43] We are assuming here that there was always a queen/first wife in Assyria and that only one person held the office at a time.[44] It seems certain that the queen was the mother of the crown prince or, if he had not yet been formally named, the mother of the eldest living son of the king, i.e., the heir apparent.[45] The real difficulty here is that we are not sure whether the term MÍ.É.GAL was only used by the queen or whether it could be used by other harem women as well (women who had borne the king children, for instance). Even if this was the case, it probably does not complicate the issue a great deal, because harem women do not seem to have owned property outside the palace (thus the economic documents mentioning a MÍ.É.GAL refer to the queen) and probably just used the term on private possessions, such as jewelry, or on votive offerings.[46]

We are faced with a similar problem with the term *mār šarri*. The commonly accepted interpretation of the phrase *mār šarri* is that it may refer either generally to any one of the king's sons or specifically to the crown prince; thus when *mār šarri* stands alone it refers to the crown prince but when a personal name accompanies the phrase it may be translated literally "son of the king." Recently, this theory has been seriously challenged by Kwasman and Parpola who prefer crown prince as the normal meaning of *mār šarri*.[47] There are many difficulties with their interpretation, not the least of which is that it results in Sennacherib having no less than four crown princes

---

42 Grayson, *CAH* III/2: 138 n. 163. See Frahm, *Sanherib*: 184-85, for a discussion of the difficulties involved in attributing the text to one of Sennacherib's wives.

43 Nothing concrete is known about Neo-Assyrian succession practices. See Porter, *Images*: 15, n. 22, for a summary of our knowledge. We know even less about the marriage practices of the Neo-Assyrian kings, but see Kuhrt, *ANE*: 526-29 for a review of the evidence.

44 We cannot discount the probability that other women in the harem held the affections of the king and from time to time gained some power by such means, but it is most unlikely that they ever dislodged the mother of the crown prince/heir apparent from her position.

45 S. Dalley and J.N. Postgate, *The Tablets from Fort Shalmaneser*. CTN 3 (London, 1984): 11.

46 See for example, the jewelry and inscriptions from the Nimrud graves. All of these "queens" may not have been of the first rank, especially the one who was an adolescent when she died. For information about the graves and their occupants see Harrak, *CMS Bulletin* 20, (1990): 5-14; A. Fadhil, "Die in Nimrud/Kalḫu aufgefundene Grabinschrift der Jabâ," *BaM* 21 (1990): 461-70; A. Fadhil, "Die Grabinschrift der Mullissu-mukannišat-Ninua aus Nimrud/Kalḫu und andere in ihrem Grab gefundene Schriftträger," *BaM* 21 (1990): 471-82.

47 Kwasman and Parpola, *SAA* VI: xxviii.

during his reign and always two holding the office simultaneously,[48] a situation which is never explicitly stated in the records. Until solid evidence can be produced to the contrary, I will assume that the eldest son of the king was considered the "heir apparent" but had to be formally inducted into the *bēt rēdūti* (that is, he had to have been approved by the gods) in order to be crown prince. By this argument, Sennacherib's son, Aššur-nadin-šumi was his only formally designated crown prince until Esarhaddon was named to the office sometime in c. 683.[49]

Four dated legal documents from this period illustrate the problem. These texts mention officers of the queen but do not identify her by name. *SAA* VI, 135 dates to 694 and therefore must refer to the mother of Aššur-nadin-šumi. *SAA* VI, 90 dates to 683 and thus could refer to Naqia, since it is around this time that Esarhaddon was named crown prince. However, *SAA* VI, 164 (and probably *SAA* VI, 165 on the grounds that the witness list is identical) dates to 686, some eight years after the disappearance of Aššur-nadin-šumi but about three years before Esarhaddon was named crown prince. This text does not refer to Naqia, but may represent either the mother of Aššur-nadin-šumi or the mother of the king's surviving eldest son, Urad-Mullissu, assuming that he was then considered to be heir apparent. However, there is no reason to believe that Aššur-nadin-šumi's mother would have had to "step down" in favor of Urad-Mullissu's mother, who may not have been of the highest rank. Once again we are faced with a frustrating lack of evidence concerning Neo-Assyrian matrimonial practices. Nevertheless, the following evidence may allow us to draw a tentative conclusion about the problem of Naqia's status.

NARGD 34-36 (= *SAA* XII, 21-23) is a grant (date not preserved) by Sennacherib in which he apparently transfers the estate of the queen mother at Šabbu to the mother of the crown prince.[50] The grant has been pieced

---

[48] Kwasman and Parpola claim that Aššur-nadin-šumi was not the crown prince of Assyria at all, that Urad-Mullissu held that post and that after the death of Aššur-nadin-šumi, a third brother Nergal-šumu-[ibni] was made crown prince of Babylon, although there is only circumstantial evidence for this (*SAA* VI: xxxiii). While we are well aware of the precedent for having a crown prince of Assyria and a crown prince of Babylon (Ashurbanipal and Šamaš-šumu-ukin), we must remember that according to *SAA* X, 185, theirs was an entirely innovative situation, i.e., a double princeship had never happened before. Since Aššur-nadin-šumi is listed in the Babylonian Chronicle as king in Babylon (Grayson, *TCS* 5: 77, Chron. I, ii 30-31), and since the period 689-681, following the destruction of Babylon, is given as "rulerless" in the Babylonian Chronicle (Grayson, *TCS* 5: 81, Chron. I, iii 28), we must conclude that no other Assyrian prince was crown prince/king of Babylon after 694 unless it was a purely notional title.

[49] Although Esarhaddon was promoted over his older brothers, we must remember that the eldest son – the one who apparently had a traditional claim to the throne – was dead. We cannot assume that in Assyria there was any formal rule of succession beyond this (comparable to modern day England, for example). On the contrary, it seems that there were no rules to govern the contingency of the death of the first born. If the mother of Aššur-nadin-šumi had no other male offspring, it may be that Sennacherib's other sons made claim to rank by age alone. We simply do not know.

[50] Postgate, *NARGD* : 70-72 and Kataja and Whiting, *SAA* XII: 22-24.

together from three different fragments which are not well preserved and it is not absolutely certain that they belong together: fragment *SAA* XII, 21 is only the introduction containing the name of Sennacherib, broken titles and the royal seal and the end containing the beginning of the date; *SAA* XII, 22 concerns extispicy performed with regards to land in the town of Šabbu, the town of the Queen Mother; and *SAA* XII, 23 is a very fragmentary text in which people are exempted from taxes and something is done for the mother of the crown prince.

Although Kataja and Whiting regard these pieces as possibly belonging to a grant for the Adad temple in Šabbu,[51] it seems that some property transfer between the queen mother and the mother of the crown prince has also occured. The transfer presumably took place after the death of the queen mother, whom we know to have been alive in 692, as shown by *SAA* VI, 143. Sennacherib's first crown prince, Aššur-nadin-šumi, on the other hand, was captured and killed in 694. Thus the question arises whether Sennacherib gave this land to Aššur-nadin-šumi's mother, to Naqia or to another wife. The answer may be found in the fact that the text refers to the receiver of this land grant not as MÍ.É.GAL (queen) but very specifically as AMA-*šú ša* DUMU LUGAL *ša* É *re*-[*du-ti*], literally "the mother of the king's son of the succession house." Since Aššur-nadin-šumi was dead when the text was written, it is surely safe to fill in the break with the name of Esarhaddon, the only other positively identified crown prince of Sennacherib. The fact that the *bēt rēdūti* is mentioned indicates that the son in question has actually been formally designated heir. This definitely points to Esarhaddon, who may have had no obvious claim to the throne (being the youngest son), but required the formality of the *bēt rēdūti* to lend him legitimacy.[52] The text emphasizes the official position of the crown prince which suggests that the promotion was recent and that the crown prince's mother benefited as a direct result of her son's advancement. Naqia is *not* called "queen" here but only the mother of the crown prince. Thus it is possible that she was not "first wife" and that someone else (Aššur-nadin-šumi's mother?) held that rank. This document may represent the protocol for dealing with the estates of the deceased queen mother, and the rest of her wealth was probably dispersed in a similar manner. Although the text shows that Naqia was given control over an estate, thus enhancing her economic status, we must remember that this occurred *after* Esarhaddon had been named crown prince.

Unfortunately there is no way to determine whether Aššur-nadin-šumi's mother retained her position in the harem, whether Naqia gained enough power to displace her before Esarhaddon was named to the succession house (although in light of *SAA* XII, 21-23 this seems unlikely), whether someone else was first lady in the harem in between, or whether Naqia displaced the

---

[51] Kataja and Whiting, *SAA* XII: xxii, xxiv-xxv.

[52] In fact Sennacherib went to great lengths to secure Esarhaddon's promotion. He imposed a loyalty oath on behalf of his son (*SAA* II, 2), apparently changed his name (see above, p. 17, n. 28) and conferred upon him the new title *mār šarri* (*rabû*) *ša bēt rēduti* which we find used in this text.

queen when Esarhaddon was chosen heir. Be that as it may, there is currently no evidence that Naqia became queen before Esarhaddon was crown prince, or that she was especially powerful or privileged.

The most likely scenario for the interval between the death of Aššur-nadin-šumi and the designation of Esarhaddon as crown prince is that the mother of Aššur-nadin-šumi simply retained her position. Urad-Mullissu may have expected to enter the *bēt rēdūti* since he was the next eldest son, but just as there is no evidence that he was ever formally designated crown prince, there is no evidence that his mother (if different from the queen) became first wife. Kwasman and Parpola argue that Urad-Mullissu was not only crown prince but had been so designated as early as 698.[53] Their argument lacks proof and, indeed, it is extremely unlikely that if Urad-Mullissu had been the official crown prince of Assyria for fifteen years he could have been expelled (without being executed) in favor of the king's youngest son. Given the fact that he was still allowed to remain at court after Esarhaddon's advancement, swore an oath of fealty to the new crown prince, and had enough access to the king to cause trouble for him,[54] it is difficult to see how he could possibly ever have been crown prince himself. It is likely, however, that Urad-Mullissu *expected* to be made crown prince, enjoyed at least some of the privileges of the office and publicly acted as if he already was the designated heir. It must have been quite a shock when, eleven years after the death of Aššur-nadin-šumi, Sennacherib finally designated an heir and it was not he. We need look no further for the murderer's primary motive in any case.[55]

The choice of Esarhaddon to be crown prince is not an immediately obvious one for two reasons. First, he was the youngest son of the king.[56] Second, there is evidence that even as crown prince (and presumably before) he exhibited symptoms of the chronically debilitating illness which was ultimately to kill him.[57] Why would Sennacherib choose his youngest, apparently weak, son to succeed him? Most scholars have simply assumed that Naqia had such influence over Sennacherib by this time that she convinced him to do this unprecedented deed.[58] Note for example, Lewy's comment, "... it is easy to see that this fateful decision (which, as is well known, was the ultimate cause of Sennacherib's assassination) was inspired into him by a woman ...,"[59] Reade's remark, "Naqia/Zakutu has long been recognized as responsible for the promotion of her own son Esarhaddon to the position of crown-

53 Kwasman and Parpola, *SAA* VI: xxxii.

54 Borger, *Asarh.*, 41, §27, Nin A, Ep. 2: 26-33 and below pp. 23-24.

55 This is not to say that other factors were not involved in the conspiracy. See P. Machinist's comments in his review of *Death in Mesopotamia,* edited by B. Alster, Mesopotamia 8 (Copenhagen, 1980), *JAOS* 104 (1984): 570.

56 Borger, *Asarh.*, 40, §27, Nin A, Ep. 2: i 8-19.

57 *SAA* X, 328 obv. 15f, refers to a bout of illness when Esarhaddon was crown prince.

58 Grayson, *CAH* III/2: 121, even suggests that "the role of the harem in political affairs under the leadership of Naqi'a" provided one of the motives for the murder of Sennacherib.

59 Lewy, *JNES* 11: 271-72.

prince late in Sennacherib's reign ...,"[60] and Leichty's assertion that "There can be little doubt that the hand of Naqi'a was behind this appointment."[61] Before we attribute such a program to Naqia, we should seriously question this assumption. After all, according to our assessment of the period 694-683, Naqia did not achieve first wife status until Esarhaddon became crown prince. It is even possible that she never became first wife at all. Naqia is not called MÍ.É.GAL in *SAA* XII, 23 and this may have been done deliberately to distinguish her from the holder of the title. In fact there is no text identifying Naqia by name and title that securely dates to Sennacherib's reign. All objects/texts which include her name date securely to either Esarhaddon's or Ashurbanipal's reigns.[62] She certainly was a MÍ.É.GAL in the sense that she was part of the "harem," but we must remember that there are two texts that give Tašmetum-šarrat the same title. What then can we conclude about Naqia's position prior to Esarhaddon's promotion? At present it seems best to be cautious in assigning Naqia any role other than that of "palace woman."

When Esarhaddon was promoted he supplanted Urad-Mullissu from a position he had enjoyed for as many as eleven years. While it is safe to assume that Naqia supported Esarhaddon's advancement, the supposition that she was somehow entirely responsible for it is not only unsupported by evidence, but excludes Esarhaddon from taking an active role in his own future. Naqia was not, after all, acting on behalf of a minor – by 683 Esarhaddon would have been roughly thirty and both Sennacherib and Naqia would have been fairly old by the standards of the day. We must look for a combination of factors to explain Sennacherib's choice of heir, not the least of which must be Esarhaddon's own merits. In addition, there were probably compelling reasons for Sennacherib not to choose any of Esarhaddon's elder brothers, although at this point any reason we might suggest would be mere speculation.[63]

That Sennacherib's choice of heir caused a great deal of internal strife which ultimately led to his murder is well known. Larsen points out that in one Assyrian text the eponym for the year 681 is given as "the eponymy after Nabû-šarru-uṣur" thus indicating that the trouble resulting from Esarhaddon's appointment interfered with the government to the point that an eponym was not assigned at the right time.[64] Sennacherib must have been aware of

---

[60] Reade, *CRRAI* 33 (1986): 142.

[61] Leichty, *CANE*: 951.

[62] The only text that does not include Esarhaddon's name and title is an inscribed bead published by Scheil in 1898. The bead was in a private collection and it is not possible to tell from Scheil's publication whether the entire text reads [f]*na-qi-ʾa-a* MÍ.É.GAL *šá* [m]30-P[AP.MEŠ-SU or it is broken. The bead itself seems to be untraceable at present.

[63] Note, however, Parpola's comment that Esarhaddon was quite possibly the only son born after Sargon II had usurped the throne and thus the only truly "royal" offspring of Sennacherib (*SAA* IX: xliii and note 206). While not a position that could have been used to displace a first born son (Aššur-nadin-šumi), such an argument might well have been put forward when Esarhaddon was promoted over his older brothers.

[64] M.T. Larsen, "Unusual Eponymy-Datings from Mari and Assyria," *RA* 68 (1974): 22, referring to *SAA* VI, 197 (= *ADD* 213). Note however *SAA* VI, 193 (= *ADD* 277) in

the discord that his decision might cause, but felt that he could contain it by imposing a loyalty oath.[65] He must have been satisfied with the results, for he does not appear to have been completely estranged from his other sons, who remained in close enough contact with him to cause trouble for Esarhaddon. Thus, Esarhaddon tells us that,

> *lišān lemut-tim kar-ṣi taš-qir-ti ki-i la lìb-bi*
> *ilāni*^meš *eli-ia ú-šab-šu-ma sur-ra-a-ti la*
> *šal-ma-a-ti arki-ia id-da-nab*^?*-bu-bu ze-ra-a-ti*
> *pa-áš-ru lìb-bi abi-ia šá la ilāni*^meš *ú-ze-en-nu-u*
> *itti-ia šap-la-a-nu lìb-ba-šu re-e-mu ra-ši-šu-ma*
> *a-na e-peš šarru-ti-ia šit-ku-na ēnā*^II*-šu*[66]
>
> Evil rumors, calumny they started against me – against the will of the gods – they were constantly repeating evil, incorrect and hostile (rumors) behind my back. They alienated from me – against the gods – the warm heart of my father, (though) at the bottom of his heart there was love (for me) and his intentions were that I should become king.

Parpola suggests that the "rumors" spread by Esarhaddon's brothers had to do with his poor health,[67] but if his condition was already chronic it can hardly have been kept secret, even if it was not widely known. It is possible, of course, that Esarhaddon suffered a bout of illness at this time, thus providing his brothers with a convenient complaint against him.[68] The role of Sennacherib's officials in all of this is not clear. However, the fact that two of his top advisors (Nabû-šumu-iškun and Ṣillâ) were apparently on Urad-Mullissu's side but managed to retain their positions into Esarhaddon's reign,[69] is undoubtedly significant, as some of the "rumors" probably reached Sennacherib through these men who were assumed to be loyal.

By roughly Nisan 681[70] the situation had deteriorated to the point that Sennacherib took action and sent Esarhaddon away to the west, either for safety's sake[71] or in exile.[72] Scholars do not agree on this point but Esarhad-

---

which the new eponym (Nabû-aḫḫe-ereš) was in place by 12.II.681, a scant week after the date of *SAA* VI, 197.

65 Parpola and Watanabe, *SAA* II, 3.

66 Borger, *Asarh.*, 41, §27, Nin A, Ep. 2: 26-31.

67 Parpola, *LAS* 2: 235.

68 Parpola, *SAA* X, 328 obv. 15-18: LUGAL *be-lí* ⌜*ki*^!*-i*^!⌝ DUMU.LUGAL *šu-tu-u-ni* [*ina x x* ^m]⌜^d?⌝PA^!*-u-a il-lik-u-ni* [*ki-i*^? *ša*^? LUG]AL^!*-ma ḫu-un-ṭu* [*ina* ŠÀ *e*]*-na-a-te uk-ti-il*$_5$ (when the king my lord was crown prince and went to ...-Nabû'a, a fever stayed in his eyes as in those of the king.)

69 *ABL* 1091 for which see Parpola, *Murderer*.

70 Parpola, *Murderer* n. 41.

71 R. Labat, "Asarhaddon et la ville de Zaqqap," *RA* 53 (1959): 113-18.

72 See Frame, *Babylonia*: 63-64.

don's account seems to indicate that Sennacherib sent him away in disfavor,[73] although the king did nothing during the approximately nine month exile to change the succession.

But what of Naqia during this period? Building on the assumption that Naqia was powerful even before she became first wife, some scholars maintain that as queen she wielded unprecedented power. Lewy even goes so far as to propose that Naqia governed Babylonia toward the end of Sennacherib's reign,[74] but this theory has no basis in fact and must be rejected.[75] Reade suggests that Sennacherib, probably as a reflection of his religious reforms, gave new status to the queen.[76] Thus, the god Aššur appears with a consort (Mullissu) at this time and, reflecting this, the king appears with his queen, as on the Louvre bronze relief. She is fully integrated into the religious rite. There are several problems with this theory, however. First of all we do not know what role queens normally played in state religious ceremonies, though it is probable that they traditionally took part in some of them.[77] Further, too little is known of Sennacherib's religious reorganization or the effects it may have had at court for us to state that the king gave the queen an expanded role in religious (or secular) activities. However, if such was the case, we have no way to determine whether the queen's elevated position was a by-product of the religious changes or vice versa.

The chief difficulty with Reade's theory, which he admits, is that the relief cannot be dated to Sennacherib's reign with certainty because the name of the king is not preserved in the inscription. Börker-Klähn attributes the bronze to Sennacherib[78] based on its supposed link to another bronze relief fragment in the Iraq Museum[79] whose inscription is said to be a Sennacherib text (figure 2).[80] However, she mistakenly cites Grayson as the source for the pairing of the bronzes, when in fact he never mentions the Louvre bronze at all.[81] If Grayson is correct in his identification of the inscription on the Iraq bronze, then the two bronzes do not belong together, for their inscriptions certainly do not. The Iraq Museum bronze describes renovations done to

---

[73] Esarhaddon's annals are not clear on this matter but only say that the gods caused him to go to a secret place where they protected him (Borger, *Asarh.*, 42, §27, Nin A, Ep. 2: i 35-40).

[74] Lewy, *JNES* 11: 272-77.

[75] See R. Borger rev. of *BBEA*, *BiOr* 29 (1972): 33-34.

[76] Reade, *CRRAI* 33 (1986): 142.

[77] See Menzel, *Tempel*: 295f.

[78] J. Börker-Klähn, *ABVF*: nos. 220-21.

[79] F. Basmachi, "Miscellanea in the Iraq Museum," *Sumer* 18 (1962): 48, fig. 1.

[80] In a letter to Dr. Basmachi published in *Sumer* 19 (1963): 111-12, Grayson identifies the inscription on the Iraq bronze as a duplicate of a Sennacherib building inscription concerning the temple Ehursaggalkurkurra at Assur. See Luckenbill, *Sennacherib:* 144-47. See also Frahm, *Sanherib*: 169-70.

[81] Börker-Klähn, *ABVF:* 214. E.A. Braun-Holzinger, *Figürliche Bronzen aus Mesopotamien,* (Munich, 1984): 105, makes the same mistake. Grayson identifies the inscription on the Iraq bronze only.

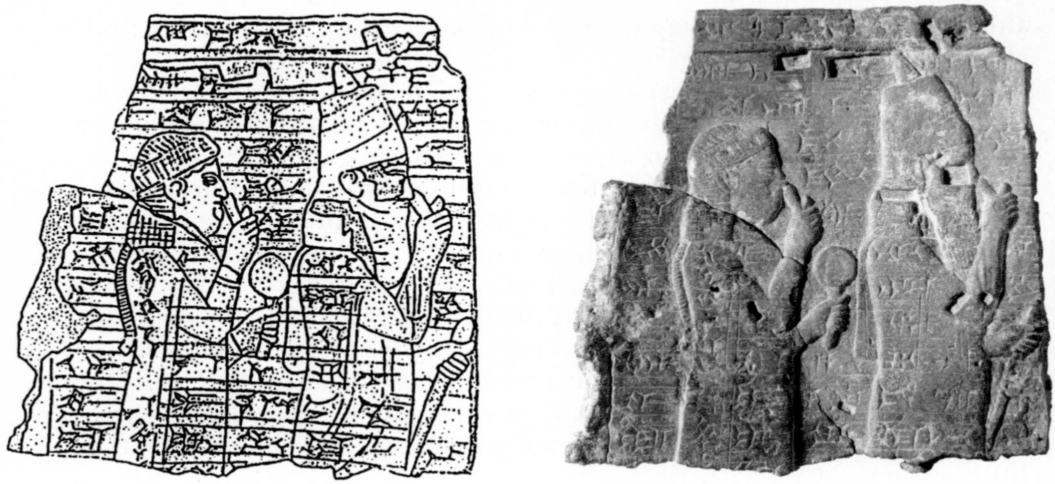

Fig. 1 Fragment of a bronze relief depiciting Naqia and the king (Esarhaddon).
(A) Line drawing (after Börker-Klähn, *ABVF*: 220)
(B) Photograph (AO 20.185; courtesy Musée du Louvre)

Ehursaggalkurkurra at Assur, while the inscription on the Naqia bronze resembles the mouth opening ceremonies described in Esarhaddon's AsBb texts.[82] The Sennacherib text to which the Iraq bronze belongs contains no comparable passage.[83]

Although the pieces seem comparable in terms of style and figure size (see Fig. 1 and 2), no chemical analysis has been made, nor accurate measurements taken to prove that they belong together. Similarity in style need not indicate that the bronzes were made at the same time, while comparable dimensions may simply show that they belonged to the same type of monument (a dais or throne base, for example) rather than to the same monument. Parrot and Nougayrol's argument for attributing the Naqia bronze to Esarhaddon remains most convincing.

Two seal impressions from Sennacherib's palace at Nineveh are also relevant. The composition of these seals is very like that of the bronze relief: the queen (identified by her hair and crown) stands behind the king worshipping a goddess.[84] However, there is no way to date these seal impressions and they might not depict Naqia. Until their discovery, the Naqia bronze seemed unique (and, as a monumental piece, it remains so), but it is possible that this composition represents the standard illustration of the queen and that other such sculptures await discovery. At present we do not believe that either the Naqia bronze or the seal impressions may be convincingly used to argue that

[82] Parrot and Nougayrol, *Syria* 33: 151-53. For the AsBb texts see Borger, *Asarh.*: 78-92.

[83] Luckenbill, *Sennacherib:* 144-47.

[84] BM 84789 and BM 84802, published by Reade in *CRRAI* 33 (1986): 144f.

Naqia held a particularly powerful position as Sennacherib's queen.

For Naqia Esarhaddon's appointment must have seemed ideal: the future was assured for her and her son. When, in the subsequent months, the situation began to change and opposition to the nomination started to gain momentum, naturally she would have striven to counteract the negative reports about Esarhaddon that were reaching the king. That she was not entirely successful in doing so may indicate that she did not have as much influence on Sennacherib as has previously been assumed. On the other hand, in spite of growing pressure, Sennacherib did not change the succession, and this may be a point in favor of Naqia's influence.

Naqia, evidently stymied in her efforts to restore Esarhaddon to Sennacherib's good graces, resorted to extispicy, astrology and oracles for favorable signs. In a letter written to Esarhaddon just a couple of months after his accession,[85] Bel-ušezib complains that Esarhaddon has abandoned him even though he remained loyal to the crown prince and,

> *it-tu šá* LUGAL-*ú-ti šá* ^md^*aš-šur*-ŠEŠ-SUM-*na* DUMU LUGAL *be-lí-*[*ia*] *a-na* ^m^*da-da-a* LÚ.MAŠ.MAŠ *ù* AMA.MAN *aq-bu-ú*
>
> I told the omen of the kingship of Esarhaddon the crown prince, my lord, to Dadâ, the exorcist, and to the mother of the king.

Although this omen must have bolstered the morale of Esarhaddon's supporters it may have prompted Urad-Mullissu and his faction to act. Esarhaddon's absence only created a stalemate for his brothers: their rival had been removed but the succession remained unchanged. In fact, the omen probably

---

85 Parpola, *SAA* X, 109. For the date of this letter see Labat, *RA* 53 (1959) and Parpola, *Murderer*, n. 41. See also the extensive discussion in Nissinen, *SAAS* 7 (1998): 89-95.

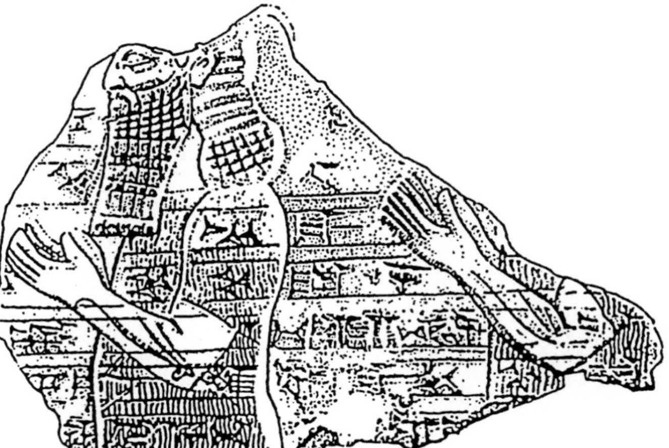

Fig. 2 Fragment of a bronze relief with two male figures.
(IM 62197; courtesy Iraq Museum, Baghdad [line drawing after Börker-Klähn, *ABVF*: 221])

improved Esarhaddon's position. By waiting, the brothers could not achieve anything, so they opted for action. On the 20th of Tebet, 681 Esarhaddon's brother(s) murdered their father and attempted to take the throne.[86]

Naqia and the rest of Esarhaddon's supporters must have kept in close contact with him while he was absent from court. When Sennacherib was killed, Esarhaddon was immediately apprised of what had occurred and while returning to Nineveh, successfully met the opposing forces of his brothers who were subsequently forced to flee and are never mentioned by Esarhaddon again. There must have been a fair amount of "cleaning up" to do back at Nineveh and elsewhere in Assyria, and Esarhaddon did not ascend the throne until about six weeks after the murder of his father. It is probably to this interval that we can date some of the oracles concerning Esarhaddon, especially the oracle from Aḫat-abiša to Naqia which explicitly refers to the period of Esarhaddon's exile:

a-na-ku ^{d}*be-let arba-ìl*
a-na AMA.LUGAL
ki-i ta-ḫu-ri-ni-ni
ma-a ša ZAG
ša šu-me-li
ina su-ni-ki ta-sak-ni
ma-a ia-ú
ṣi-it ŠÀ-*bi-ia*
EDIN *tu-sar-pi-di*
ú-ma-a LUGAL *la ta-pa-làḫ*
LUGAL-*tú ik-ku-u*
da-na-nu ik-ku-u-ma
ša pi-i ^{MÍ}NIN.AD-*šá*
DUMU.MÍ ^{URU}*arba-ìl*

I am the Lady of Arbela. To the king's mother: Because you implored me saying "You have placed the ones at the (king's) right and left side in your lap, but made my own offspring roam the steppe" Now fear not, (my) king! The kingdom is yours, yours is the power. By the mouth of the woman Aḫat-abiša of Arbela.[87]

The fact that several oracles[88] were consulted by Naqia and Esarhaddon around the time of his accession reveals the severity of the situation and

---

86 B. Landsberger and Th. Bauer, "Zu neuveröffentlichen Geschichtsquellen der Zeit von Asarhaddon bis Nabonid," *ZA* 37 (1927): 65ff, claim that Esarhaddon (with the complicity of his mother) was Sennacherib's murderer. Recently Parpola (*Murderer*) has identified the chief villain as Urad-Mullissu (named Adramelech in the Bible: 2 Kings 19 and Isaiah 37) and Esarhaddon has been exonerated.

87 Transliteration and translation from S. Parpola, *SAA* IX, 1.8.

88 See M. Weippert, "Assyrische Prophetien der Zeit Asarhaddons und Assurbanipals," *ARINH*: 94ff, S. Parpola, *SAA* IX, 1.8, 5, and Nissinen, *SAAS* 7: 22-29.

shows that Naqia was as concerned with prognostication as her son. Esarhaddon also imposed a loyalty oath at this time.[89] This *adê* agreement is particularly interesting because Esarhaddon, who is referred to in the text only as 'my lord,' thus indicating that he was not yet king, imposes the oath himself without the patronage of his mother. It is evident that in 681, although the need for it was greater, Naqia did not have the power or status to impose an oath on behalf of her son, as she was later to do in 669 on behalf of her grandson.

In this chapter we have examined the evidence for Naqia's origins, for her rise to power in Sennacherib's harem, for the role she played in the promotion of her son to crown prince and subsequent events at court. As we have seen, there is very little solid evidence for any of these things, but a careful examination of the sources allows us to draw some conclusions. The name Naqia is West Semitic but the evidence does not allow us to say where she came from or how she entered the harem. We know that after Esarhaddon became crown prince she acquired property (in Šabbu) and probably further wealth and power. However, it is unlikely that she gained first wife status much before Esarhaddon was named crown prince and may, in fact, have achieved this position (officially) only as a result of his nomination if at all. Naqia undoubtedly strove to promote and sustain the position of her son but cannot be seen to have been entirely responsible for his success. There may be evidence (the questionably dated bronze relief) that as Sennacherib's queen she achieved an unprecedented position, but at this point, such a supposition is conjecture. Naqia probably played a secondary role in the events surrounding the murder of Sennacherib (i.e., tried to bolster her son's position and kept him well apprised of the situation through continuous communications) but did not actively take part.

The image we have of Naqia during this early stage in her career does not correspond to that of other scholars who claim that Naqia had overwhelming influence on both her husband and her son. The picture we have is more conservative. None of the evidence would lead us to conclude that during this period Naqia held more power than was normal for a queen/palace woman. Indeed, when Esarhaddon was in trouble her only recourse seems to have been to consult oracles on his behalf. It is a testimony to Esarhaddon's wit, ability and perseverance that in spite of strong opposition, he finally attained his objective and was able to ascend the throne after a short, but not entirely successful, civil war (the culprits were not apprehended).

CHAPTER III

IMAGE AS POLITICAL TOOL:
MAKING THE QUEEN MOTHER AN AUTHORITY FIGURE

When Esarhaddon successfully ascended the throne of Assyria, Naqia became queen mother, the highest rank a woman could achieve. Nearly all the sources that concern her date to Esarhaddon's reign, and while they are fragmentary and sometimes ambiguous, they suggest that, as queen mother, Naqia enjoyed a special status. The nature and source of Naqia's power have yet to be fully defined, however.

Our view of Naqia is of necessity related to our understanding of Esarhaddon and the political events of his reign. Until recently, Esarhaddon has generally been seen as a "weak and vacillating" king whose superstitious fears made it easy for his advisors to manipulate him.[1] If Esarhaddon is viewed in this way it is natural to see Naqia as a domineering queen mother who became the "power behind the throne." Thus it has been suggested that she governed Babylonia for her son, was instrumental in the reconstruction of Babylon[2] and was responsible for choosing Ashurbanipal as crown prince.[3]

However, recent scholarship has shown that Esarhaddon was an intelligent and able king whose advisors competed to retain his favor.[4] Although his reign was comparatively short (eleven years as compared to his father's

---

[1] See most especially A.T.E. Olmstead, *History of Assyria* (Chicago: University of Chicago Press, 1923): 347; W. von Soden, *Herrscher im alten Orient,* Verständliche Wissenschaft, Bd. 54 (Berlin, Göttingen, and Heidelberg: Springer-Verlag, 1954): 125; B. Landsberger, *Brief des Bischofs von Esagila an König Asarhaddon,* Mededeelingen der Koninklijke Nederlandse Akademie van Wetenschappen, Afd. Letterkunde, Nieuwe Reeks, Deel 28 No 6 (Amsterdam Noord-Hollandische Uitgevers Maatschappij, 1965): 14; R. Labat, "Das Assyrische Reich unter den Sargoniden," *Fischer Weltgeschichte* 4, edited by E. Cassin, J. Bottéro and J. Vercoutter (Frankfurt am Main: Fischer Bücherei, 1967): 81; and J.A. Brinkman, *Prelude to Empire: Babylonian Society and Politics, 747-626 B.C.,* Occasional Publications of the Babylonian Fund, 7 (Philadelphia: The University Museum, 1984): 71 (where he calls Esarhaddon "impressionable and valetudinarian").

[2] See for example, Parrot and Nougayrol, *Syria* 33 (1956):157; Lewy, *JNES* 11 (1952): 277, and Reade, *CRRAI* 33 (1986):142.

[3] Z. Ben-Barak, "The Queen Consort and the Struggle for the Succession to the Throne," *CRRAI* 33 (1986): 37 and E. Leichty, *CANE*: 956.

[4] In particular see Parpola, *LAS* 2: XVIIIff and *passim*, and Porter, *Images*: 2-3.

twenty-four), he managed to impose the *pax Assyriaca* on most of the empire and extend its borders to include Egypt.[5] Esarhaddon's reconstruction of Babylon and the implementation of a positive policy that brought lasting peace to Babylonia reveal that he was an astute statesman – by no means the dupe of his advisors.[6] It is true that Esarhaddon was deeply concerned with religious matters, especially prognostication and divining the will of the gods, but in the context of Assyrian culture and religion, this should not be seen as a weakness.[7]

If a reassessment of Esarhaddon leads to the conclusion that he was indeed an able and intelligent king who acted decisively and competently, then surely it is not safe simply to assume that his mother was the real power behind the throne. We must adjust our view of Naqia's role at court accordingly. If Naqia wielded real power during the reign of her son it can only be because Esarhaddon sanctioned it. In the last chapter we saw that Naqia did not play an active role in the events leading up to her son's accession. She did not, therefore, start her son's reign from an established position of great authority. There is no reason that Esarhaddon would have had to put up with his mother's interference when he was king. If he had not wanted her to be powerful he could simply have confined her to the palace or one of her estates.

Yet the sources do suggest that Naqia wielded authority when Esarhaddon was king. She built a palace for Esarhaddon at Nineveh,[8] dedicated cult objects,[9] received letters from high officials in Assyria and Babylonia,[10] was depicted on at least one relief,[11] had her image portrayed on a statue[12] and was referred to by Esarhaddon's advisors with accolades normally reserved for kings alone.[13] For example, Marduk-šakin-šumi writes to the king: ^{MÍ}AMA LUGAL [*k*]*i*$^{!}$-*i a-da-pi* [*t*]*a*$^{!}$-*la-ʾi-i* (the mother of the king is capable as

---

[5] Esarhaddon was not entirely successful in his efforts to maintain the empire and he apparently lost territory in Anatolia (Grayson, *CAH* III/2: 127.) His control of Egypt was not firm for the situation there required him to launch another campaign in 669. Since Esarhaddon died on this campaign it was left to Ashurbanipal to reconquer Egypt.

[6] For discussion of his Babylonian policy see Landsberger, *BBEA;* J.A. Brinkman, "Through a Glass Darkly: Esarhaddon's Retrospects on the Downfall of Babylon," *JAOS* 103 (1983): 35-42; Brinkman, *Prelude*: 70-84; M. Cogan, "Omens and Ideology in the Babylonian Inscriptions of Esarhaddon," *HHI*: 76-84; Frame, *Babylonia*: 64-101; and Porter, *Images*.

[7] S. Parpola, *Letters from Assyrian Scholars to the Kings Esarhaddon and Assurbanipal. Part IIA: Introduction and Appendixes,* dissertation, University of Helsinki (Kevelaer, Neukirchen-Vluyn, 1971): 47, Parpola, *LAS* 2: 235, and Nissinen, SAAS 7: 90-91.

[8] Borger, *Asarh.*, 116, §86.

[9] Kohler and Ungnad, *ARU* 14; Van De Mieroop, *Hallo Fest.*: 259-61.

[10] The Assyrian letters are *SAA* XIII, 76 and 77, *SAA* X, 16 and 17, and *CT* 53, 182 and 921. The Babylonian letters are *ABL* 254 and 917, and *SAA* X, 154 and 313.

[11] The Louvre bronze relief on which she is depicted standing behind a king (Fig. 1, p. 26). See Parrot and Nougayrol, *Syria* 33 and Börker-Klähn, *ABVF*, 220 and 221.

[12] *SAA* XIII, 61 rev. 3-5.

[13] Parpola, *LAS* 2: 176 and 231.

Adapa),[14] and Issar-šumu-ereš writes to Esarhaddon: [The verdict of the mother of the king, my lord] followed by [*ki*]-*i ša* DINGIR^{MEŠ} *ga-mer* [*b*]*é-et ta-kar-ri-bi-ni* É *ta-na-zi-ri-ni na-ze-er* (is as final as that of the gods. What you bless, is blessed. What you curse, is cursed).[15] Naqia's position was strong throughout Esarhaddon's reign. Her power cannot be viewed as the product of an overbearing personality; Esarhaddon must have allowed his mother to be important and he must have done so for a reason. By reviewing the primary problems that Esarhaddon faced during his reign, we can determine why Esarhaddon established his mother as an authority figure. We can then show how the king presented his mother to the court and public.

Having successfully quelled the rebellion following Sennacherib's murder, albeit without apprehending the murderer(s),[16] Esarhaddon ascended the throne on the 18th (or 28th[17]) of Addaru, 681. By the defeat of his brothers he had shown that he was capable of leading a successful military campaign. The circumstances of that campaign – the daring confrontation of the superior force which apparently surrendered *en masse*[18] – probably helped him establish his popularity at home and consolidate his control of the military. His moral position was unassailable: he was the legitimate heir, avenging patricide/regicide, while his brothers had not only committed a heinous crime against their father, but had also broken their sacred oath to support Esarhaddon as crown prince.[19] Nevertheless, Esarhaddon's political position when he came to the throne was precarious. The circumstances under which he became king had a lasting effect on Essarhaddon and many of his policy decisions can be directly attributed to these experiences.[20]

---

[14] *SAA* X, 244, r.7ff. For examples of comparing kings to Adapa see Parpola, *LAS* 2: 219. For the sage Adapa in Neo-Assyrian scholarly thought see Parpola, *SAA* X: xix.

[15] *SAA* X, 17, r.1ff. See Streck, *Assurbanipal*: 22, ii 123ff for an example of the potency of Ashurbanipal's curse.

[16] Esarhaddon's inscriptions do not name the country to which the brothers fled. The Bible (2 Kings 19:37 and Isaiah 37:38) says that they fled to Urartu. Esarhaddon's campaign agaist Šubria in 673 was at least partly motivated by the desire to extradite Assyrian political refugees (Borger, *Asarh.*, 102, §68, Der "Gottesbrief,": i 3) some of whom may have been involved in Sennacherib's murder or the subsequent civil war. It is even possible that his brothers were among the fugitives, although this is not stated explicitly. For discussions of the *casus belli* for the Šubrian campaign see A.L. Oppenheim, "Neo-Assyrian and Neo-Babylonian Empires," in *Propaganda and Communication in World History I: The Symbolic Instrument in Early Times,* edited by A.L. Oppenheim, H.D. Lasswell, D. Lerner and H. Speiser (Honolulu: University Press of Hawaii, 1979): 129-33; H. Tadmor, "Autobiographical Apology in the Royal Assyrian Literature," *HHI*: 43; and E. Leichty, "Esarhaddon's 'Letter to the Gods,'" *Tadmor AV*: 52-57.

[17] The Babylonian Chronicle is broken here, and there is room for another winkelhaken, so Esarhaddon's coronation could have been on Addaru 18 or 28. See Grayson, *TCS* 5: 82.

[18] Borger, *Asarh.*, 44, §27, Nin A, Ep. 2: 72-79.

[19] Esarhaddon specifically states that his brothers had sworn the loyalty oath when he became crown prince. Borger, *Asarh.*, 40, §27 Nin A and F, Ep.2: 15-17.

[20] Especially with respect to the succession. See Tadmor, *HHI*: 44-45.

As king, Esarhaddon had to prove himself capable of managing the political machinations of an entrenched court, some of whose members had plotted against him during the civil war. Although Esarhaddon must have acted against opposition at court with due speed, we know that at least two officials who had been involved in the conspiracy avoided detection for several years.[21] Doubt about the loyalty of his courtiers and the dependability of his allies is a theme that is constant throughout Esarhaddon's reign.[22] He evidently felt that none of his advisors could be completely trusted.

After the murder of Sennacherib, the civil war in Assyria afforded Nabû-zer-kitti-lišir, governor of the Sealand and one of the sons of Marduk-apla-iddina II, the opportunity to rebel. Although in this case the insurrection was not successful, it alerted Esarhaddon to the fact that Sennacherib's destruction of Babylon had not wholly eradicated Babylonian resistance. Thus the problem of how to rule Babylonia had not been solved, but urgently needed attention. A rebellious Babylonia drained Assyria of essential resources – men and goods – while it also deprived her of important tax revenues and meant that key trade routes were often endangered or cut off.[23] It was vital that Esarhaddon find a lasting solution to the Babylonian problem.

Given an opportunity (any perceived weakness on the part of the central government), Assyria's vassals and dependencies rebelled with alarming regularity. Within two years of Esarhaddon's accession he had to confront rebellions along the Mediterranean coast and in Asia Minor as well. A rebellion anywhere in the empire required a costly punitive campaign to extinguish it. Insurrection could not be tolerated since, left unchecked, it might spread throughout the empire.

The fear of rebellion was ever present and well founded and is intimately bound up with Esarhaddon's concern about the succession and his ability to lay the groundwork for a smooth transfer of power. When he became king his children were still young – Ashurbanipal can only have been a small boy.[24] If Esarhaddon's brothers were still at large, then they posed a constant threat to him and his children.[25] Furthermore, at least seven of Esarhaddon's off-

---

[21] In *ABL* 1091 the officials Nabû-šumu-iškun and Ṣillâ are denounced as having taken part in the conspiracy to murder Sennacherib. For this letter and a discussion of the plot to murder Sennacherib see Parpola, *Murderer*.

[22] In the period immediately preceding Esarhaddon's coronation he imposed a loyalty oath (*SAA* II, 4) which included a vow to report sedition on the part of magnates, governors, bearded officials and eunuchs (lines 4-8). Letters from one official denouncing another are quite common in the letter corpus (see for example, *SAA* X, 199, 316 and 369 and Parpola, *Iraq* 34: 31). A large number of queries concern the loyalty of officials and/or allies (*SAA* IV, 19, 20, 139, 140), and after the abortive coup attempt of 670 Esarhaddon imposed yet another loyalty oath on his officials in Assyria and Babylonia (*SAA* II, 7).

[23] Porter, *Images*: 30.

[24] Parpola, *LAS* 2: n. 390.

[25] See above, p. 33, n. 16.

spring were male[26] which, although it helped assure the succession, also meant that there was potential for internecine strife. The succession problem was actually twofold: on the one hand Esarhaddon had to defend his sons from external attempts to deny them the throne; on the other hand he had to guard against internal conspiracy.[27] Before the designation of the crown prince(s), Esarhaddon's death would almost certainly have caused civil war unless someone had enough authority to keep order as regent until the eldest son came of age.[28] Anticipating the possibility that he might die while his sons were still young, Esarhaddon included a stipulation in the so-called "Vassal Treaties" that called for oath-takers to support his sons in spite of their youth.[29] The fact that such a provision was included in these treaties, which were enacted in 672 to settle the succession, shows that Esarhaddon was worried that Ashurbanipal and Šamaš-šumu-ukin were quite young and might not be able to hold the throne without help. By itself, a loyalty oath might not be enough of a deterrent against rebellion; it had not proved effective when Esarhaddon was named crown prince. He needed someone in a position of authority, whom he could trust implicitly to impose order and see that Ashurbanipal take the throne without mishap.

Esarhaddon also had to worry about an early demise. Little is known about the king's health during the early years of his reign, but it is likely that he experienced episodes of severe illness.[30] If, as has been suggested, Esarhaddon's ill health had been effectively used as a complaint against him by his brothers when he was crown prince, he would have been aware of its potential as a dangerous propaganda tool for his enemies.[31] A sickly king was a

---

[26] Parpola, *LAS* 2: 117-18. Note Parpola's comment that as many as nineteen children can be identified in general terms.

[27] In Esarhaddon's accession treaty (*SAA* II, 4, l. 4) he explicitly includes his progeny as among those whose words and actions should be reported to the king.

The succession treaty of 672 (most recently edited in *SAA* II, 6) contains many injunctions against helping Ashurbanipal's brothers (sometimes specifically designated DUMU AMA-*šú* "his mother's sons") rebel against him.

[28] There is some difficulty about who the eldest son actually was. Šamaš-šumu-ukin states in one of his legal records that he is Esarhaddon's *māru ašarēdu* (first son). See L.A. King, *Babylonian Boundary-Stones and Memorial-Tablets in the British Museum,* (London, 1912): X obv. 9. It is possible that Sin-nadin-apli (for whom there exists a query about whether he should be chosen as crown prince [*SAA* IV, 14]), was actually Esarhaddon's eldest son who died before he could become crown prince. Parpola (*LAS* 2: 190 and the literature cited there) argues convincingly that Sin-nadin-apli was actually Ashurbanipal and that he took Ashurbanipal as a new name when he became crown prince, just as Esarhaddon had become Aššur-etel-ilani-mukin-apli when he was designated crown prince.

[29] *SAA* II, 6, §7 ll. 83ff: *šum-ma* ^{m}*aš-šur*-PAB-AŠ MAN KUR-*aš-šur ina ṣa-ha-ri šá* DUMU.MEŠ-*šú a-na šim-ti it-ta-lak* (if Esarhaddon, king of Assyria, goes to his fate while his sons are minors ...).

[30] As pointed out by Parpola, *LAS* 2: 235, "One of the reasons prompting Esarhaddon to settle the succession already in 672 – only 8 years after his own accession – almost certainly was his growing worry about his health, a painful feeling that he was 'running out of time.'"

[31] Parpola, *LAS* 2: 235.

vulnerable king. Esarhaddon had to deal with the consequences of his chronic illness. After 672, by which time his condition seems to have deteriorated, we know that Ashurbanipal took an active role in government when his father was ill.[32] Before this time the king may not have been completely incapacitated when he was ill, but he would have been acutely aware of his vulnerability. Once again (as with the succession) Esarhaddon needed someone of unquestionable loyalty in a position of authority who could make a show of strength and maintain the *status quo* when he was disabled.

Thus, when Esarhaddon became king he had not only various pressing political problems with which to contend (the aftermath of civil war in Assyria, rebellion in Babylonia, and a restless empire) but also, *from the very beginning of his reign*, a number of potentially lethal situations to prepare for and avert (conspiracy, rebellion, the succession and the consequences of his own ill health). In fact, he dealt successfully with all of these problems. We have pointed out that (with good reason) Esarhaddon did not trust either his officials or his allies. His brothers had murdered his father, which undoubtedly made Esarhaddon aware of the potential for disaster within his own family.[33] The only person he could trust unequivocally was his mother. Her position and livelihood depended entirely upon her son; if he lost the throne, she lost her power and status. There was no reason for her to betray him. In the next section of this chapter we shall show that Esarhaddon turned to Naqia and established her as an authority figure who served as a bastion of strength for him: when he was ill or on campaign Naqia could keep an eye on things; when he died she could see to it that Ashurbanipal became king.

However, the task of establishing Naqia in a position of authority was not without difficulty. Esarhaddon could not afford to appear weak or be seen to depend on his mother. Nor could he risk offending his supporters by putting a woman in authority over them. The goal had to be accomplished with subtlety, and with careful regard to protocol. The program was carried out on two levels, public and private (court),[34] and it also had a geographical

---

[32] Parpola, *SAA* X, 316 (= *LAS* 247), r.13: *pa-lu-ú ša* LUGAL DUMU.LUGAL (rule of the king [and crown] prince). For further comments on the "joint rule" see *LAS* 2: 235-36.

[33] This may be one of the reasons why we know so little about Ešarra-ḫamat, Esarhaddon's primary wife. It is possible that he felt that her first loyalty would be to her children (as his mother's had been?). On the other hand, most of Esarhaddon's letter corpus dates to the years after the queen's death, so it is possible that she was an active queen and we just don't have the evidence for it. The fact that her death was mentioned in the Babylonian Chronicle (Grayson, *TCS* 5, 85 Chron. I: 22) suggests that she was an important woman, but she may have been overshadowed by her mother-in-law. At this point we cannot say.

[34] In recent years much work has been devoted to the propaganda programs of various Neo-Assyrian kings. See for example, (on reliefs) I. Winter, "Royal Rhetoric and the Development of Historical Narrative in Neo-Assyrian Reliefs," *Studies in Visual Communications* 7 (1981) 2-38; I. Winter, "The Program of the Throneroom of Assurnasirpal II," in *Essays on Near Eastern Art and Archaeology in Honor of Charles Kyrle Wilkinson,* edited by P. Harper and H. Pittman (New York: the Metropolitan Museum of Art, 1983): 15-32; J.M. Russell, *Sennacherib's Palace without Rival at Nineveh* (Chicago and

component. Naqia had to be known to the ruling classes in various parts of the empire, not just in Assyria, although the officials closest to Esarhaddon would have been the main target of the propaganda.[35] It was important that Naqia be generally known to the public as a rich, powerful and pious woman. At court this image would be amplified: Naqia would be active and knowledgable but political/policy decisions made by the king could not be perceived as originating with the queen mother.

The public image of the imposing queen mother was relatively easy to establish. Building works and evidence that she took part in temple activities would have evinced a strong and pious character. At court, the avenues for establishing Naqia as a strong presence were more difficult to maneuver. It is likely that a protocol for the activities of queen mothers was already at least notionally in place, although this probably depended on what any given king perceived his mother's role to be.[36] Nevertheless, by careful manipulation of such media as royal inscriptions and dedicatory inscriptions, and by deliberately associating himself with his mother, Esarhaddon might accomplish the desired end.

One of the best ways to display power and wealth was to sponsor a building program of some kind. Large scale building was a key element in the activities of every Neo-Assyrian king. Each new king tried to surpass his predecessor to impress the public, the court and the gods by constructing or refurbishing grandiose palaces, temples, public works (aqueducts, quays) and military installations. Esarhaddon was well aware of the propaganda value of such a program, and from the beginning of his reign, building played a large part in his overall public relations policy.[37] His building activities in Babylonia and Assyria were carefully managed to balance each other and to reveal Esarhaddon as a strong and pious monarch, dedicated to ruling justly in both countries.[38] In Assyria, Esarhaddon carried out both secular and religious construction projects; in Babylonia his work was almost exclusively devoted to religious projects. This was intended to show that the king's interest centered

---

London: Univ. of Chicago Press, 1991); (on texts) M. Liverani, "The Ideology of the Assyrian Empire," in *Power and Propaganda: a Symposium on Ancient Empires,* edited by M.T. Larsen, Mesopotamia 7 (Copenhagen, 1979) 297-318; P. Garelli, "La propagande royale assyrienne," *Akkadica* 27 (1982): 16-29; Oppenheim, "Neo-Assyrian and Neo-Babylonian Empires," (above n. 16); and Porter, *Images* (for Esarhaddon's program in Babylonia).

[35] M. Liverani, "The Ideology of the Assyrian Empire," *Power and Propaganda*: 298-99.

[36] The previous queen mother was Sennacherib's mother, about whom almost nothing is known (see *NARGD* 34-36, *SAA* XII, 21-23 and *SAA* VI, 143).

[37] Esarhaddon began his reconstruction projects in Babylonia in the early years of his reign (Borger, *Asarh.*, 10-30, §11, Bab. A-G). For comments on the dates of his Babylonian inscriptions see H. Tadmor, "History and Ideology in the Assyrian Royal Inscriptions," *ARINH*: 22; Cogan, *HHI:* 85-87 and Porter, *Images*: 169-76. In Assyria, he worked on the *ekal māšarti* at Nineveh and Calah in the first half of his reign and also reconstructed various temples (Borger, *Asarh. passim*).

[38] Porter, *Images*: 66.

on Assyria in spite of the attention Babylonia received.[39] The projects were accompanied by inscriptions which interpreted them for various audiences (i.e., the public or court in Assyria or Babylonia).[40]

In light of Esarhaddon's continued use of building as a propaganda tool, it is not surprising that he and his mother should use it as a means for declaring Naqia's position in the kingdom. Naqia built a palace for Esarhaddon at Nineveh. The site of the palace has yet to be discovered, but in the surviving building inscription the location is given as *ina qabal ali šá Ninua*^{ki} [*ku*]-*tal*$^{!}$ *bit* ^{d}*Sin u* ^{d}*Šamaš* (in the midst of Nineveh behind the Sin and Šamaš temple).[41] As part of his own building scheme Esarhaddon rebuilt the Sin and Šamaš temple at Nineveh early in his reign.[42] Naqia's construction was probably begun after repairs to the Sin and Šamas temple were made (i.e., after 677). A further indication of the date can be found in the text itself, which bears a striking resemblance to Esarhaddon's *ekal māšarti* inscriptions,[43] the earliest of which (Nin B7) dates to 676. The later inscriptions (Nin A variety) date to 673. Thus 677 is a *terminus post quem* and 673 must be seen as the *terminus ante quem*. Naqia's palace was probably underway by about 676.

Naqia's construction of a palace for the king was unprecedented.[44] With this single act, the message of Naqia's status and authority was unambiguously presented to the public. For the court and the inner circle of advisors, it was a different matter, however. Although Esarhaddon and his mother chose the vehicle for their message wisely (building a residence would not carry the same political charge as, for instance, rebuilding a temple or constructing anything to do with the military), such an unparalleled display of the queen mother's authority might be misconstrued. Their explanation is, I believe, to be found in the surviving building inscription, which might have been read for the benefit of court dignitaries at the festivities inaugurating the palace or at some other event.[45]

---

39 Porter, *Images*: 66 and 75.

40 Porter, *Images*: 94-105 and Russell, *Sennacherib's Palace* (above n. 34): 223-40.

41 Borger, *Asarh.*, 116, §86, II: 16-17.

42 This is described in Nin G which is dated 677 (Borger, *Asarh.*, 66-67, §29, Nin G).

43 For further discussion of this see below pp. 40-41.

44 There are many examples of the king building residences for other people (the queen, the crown prince ...), but I know of no other Neo-Assyrian example of anyone building something for a king. For earlier examples of officials building for the king see W.W. Hallo, "Royal Inscriptions of Ur: a Typology." *Hebrew Union College Annual* 33 (1962): 1-43.

45 Porter, *Images*: 109ff and 112-15, discusses at length the difficulty in seeing building inscriptions as propaganda documents for contemporary audiences, and presents a variety of possible means for transmission of texts to a wider audience. I would suggest that copies of the foundation texts were read at the banquet that was customarily held when a new palace was opened, or possibly at the ceremony when the gods were invited inside – or even at both. It seems highly unlikely that so much trouble would have been taken to make building inscriptions ideologically relevant if no one would ever hear/read them. See also Russell's comments on 'audience' in *Sennacherib's Palace* (above n. 34): 223-40.

This text exists in three fragmentary copies, two of which were published as a composite by Borger.[46] It is written and organized exactly like a royal building inscription, although (and this must have been done on purpose) it is considerably shorter and less hyperbolic than royal building inscriptions. In order to appreciate fully the message contained in the text we must quote it in full here.[47]

I *[Zakutu/Naqia sinnišat] ekalli [ša Sin-aḫḫe-]eriba šar kiššati [šar māt Aššur]*^{ki} *[kal]-lat* ^{m}*[Šarru-u]kin [š]àr kiš-šá-ti [š]àr mat [Aš-š]ur*^{ki} *ummi [Aš-šur-*ŠEŠ]-SUM-*na šàr kiš-[š]á-ti šàr mat Aš-šu[r]*^{ki}*-ma* ^{d}*Aš-šur* ^{d}*Sin* ^{d}*Šamaš* ^{d}*[Nabû]* ^{d}*Marduk [Ištar ša Ninu]a*^{ki} *[Ištar ša Arba'ili]*^{ki} *[Aš-šur-*ŠEŠ]-SUM-*na* DUMU *ṣi-it lìb-bi-ia ina* ^{giš}GU.ZA AD-*šú ṭa-b[iš] dam-qu ú-še-ṣu-ú a-na r[e-šeti tam-ti]m e-li-ti a-di tam-tim šap-[li-ti] it-tal-la-ku-ma ma-ḫi-ra la i-[šu x]-e-šú*

II *...is-pu-nu*$^{!}$*-[ma] šarrāni*^{meš} *šá kib-rat erbetti id-du-u ṣer-re-e-tú nišê*^{meš} *mātāte ki-šit-ti na-ki-ri ḫu-bu-ut* ^{giš}*qašti-šú ša a-na eš-qí bēlu-ú-ti-ia iš-ru-ka* ^{giš}*al-lu tup-šik-ku ú-šá-á-áš-ši-šú-nu-ti-ma il-bi-nu libuttu qaq-qa-ru pu-ṣe-e ina qabal āli šá Ninua*^{ki} *[ku]-tal*$^{!}$ *bit* ^{d}*Sin u* ^{d}*Šamaš [ana mušab*$^{?}$*] šarru-u-ti [ša Aššur-aḫu*$^{?}$*]-iddina*(?) *[mār narām libbi*$^{?}$*]-ia...*

III *...*ŠU*...ú-šat-r[i-ṣa elišu]* ^{giš}*dalat*^{meš} ^{giš}*šurmēni šu-ta-ḫa-a-ti qiš-ti māri-ia ú-rat-ta-a babāni*^{meš} *bītu šu-a-tu ar-ṣip ú-šak-lil lu-le-e ú-ma-al-li* ^{d}*Aš-šur* ^{d}*Ninurta* ^{d}*Sin* ^{d}*Ša-maš* ^{d}*Adad* ^{d}*Nabû u* ^{d}*Marduk ilāni*^{meš} *a-ši-bu-ut Ninua*^{ki} *ina qer-bi-šú aq-re-e-ma* ^{udu}*nīqē*^{meš} *taš-r[i-i]ḫ-te eb-bu-ú-[ti maḫaršun aqqima]*

IV *... šarru [...] eli [...] mim-ma [...] x [..]* RU *[...] a-šib [...] lil-bur [...]* ^{d}*šedu [...]* ^{d}*lamassu* XX XX *qé-reb-šú ip-qí-du-ma it-ta-ru-ú ka-a-a-an Aš-šur-aḫu-idina šàr mār Aš-šur*^{ki} *mār narām lìb-bi-[ia] ina qer-[bi-šu] aq-re-e-[ma] àš-ta-[kan nigutu*$^{?}$*] ...*

V *...[...] x ú-šá-áš-kin mim-ma aq-ru ḫe-še-eḫ-ti ekalli si-mat šarru-ú-ti a-na Aš-šur-áḫu-[idina] mār [narām libbiia*$^{?}$*] ...*

Zakutu/Naqia queen of Sennacherib, king of the world, king of Assyria, daughter-in-law of Sargon, king of the world, king of Assyria, mother of Esarhaddon, king of the world, king of Assyria. Aššur, Sin, Šamaš, Nabû, Marduk, Issar of Nineveh, Issar of Arbela were pleased (and) they happily put Esarhaddon, (my) son, my own offspring, on the throne of

[46] Borger, *Asarh.*, 115-16, §86. The third fragment was discovered by Borger in 1987 (Borger, *ARRIM* 6 [1988]: 7 and 11).

[47] The transliteration is from Borger, *Asarh.*, 116, §86, and Borger, *ARRIM* 6: 11 (I have left the sumerograms to indicate which part is restored from the new fragment), with one small addition: I have restored *maḫaršun aqqima* at the end of column III. The translation is my own.

> his father. From the top of the upper sea to the lower sea they went back and forth [...] no rival.
>
> His [enemies?] they destroyed and they put the nose rope on the kings of the four quarters. People of all the lands, enemy captives that were his part of the booty, he gave as my lordly portion and I caused them to carry the hoe and the dirt basket and they made bricks. A piece of empty land in the midst of Nineveh behind the Sin and Šamas temple, for a royal residence of Esarhaddon, my beloved son ...
>
> ... I stretched across it. Door leaves of cypress, a gift of my son I hung side by side in its gates. That house I constructed, completed and filled (it) with splendor. Aššur, Ninurta, Sin, Šamaš, Adad and Issar, Nabû and Marduk, the gods who dwell in Nineveh, I invited inside and [I made before them] pure, extravagant offerings.
>
> The king ... on ... whatever ... the one who lives ... the ... *šedu* and the ... *lamassu* ... care for its interior and constantly watch over (it) ... I had set ... Esarhaddon, king of Assyria my beloved son, I invited inside and held a banquet ...
>
> Everything valuable, furnishings of a palace, symbols of kingship, for Esarhaddon, my beloved son ...

All of the standard elements of a building inscription are present in this text: introductory titulary/genealogy, description of labor and materials, location of the building, list of furnishings, sacrifice for gods, banquet and description of its lavish splendor and its purpose. It is no accident that these are topoi that are present in almost all Sargonid building inscriptions. By including these sections Naqia puts herself firmly on the level of royalty.

In fact, much of the text is written with the exact language of one of Esarhaddon's own building inscriptions, Nin B7, that describes his construction of the *ekal māšarti* at Nineveh.[48] Compare for example col. II lines 5ff of our text with Nin B7, col. V, lines 44-46:

> UKÚ.MEŠ KUR.KUR *ḫu-bu-ut* GIŠ.BAN-*ia al-lu tup-šik-ku ú-šá-áš-ši-šú-nu-ti-ma il-bi-nu* SIG$_4$.ḪI.A
>
> people of all the lands that were my share of the booty I made them carry the hoe and the dirt basket and they moulded bricks;

and col. III, lines 9ff of our text with col. VI, lines 4ff of B7:

---

48 This text (B7 was published by A. Heidel and A.L. Oppenheim, "A New Hexagonal Prism of Esarhaddon (676 B.C.)," *Sumer* 12 [1956]: 9-37) served as the basis for Nin A (Borger, *Asarh.*, 36-38, §26) which was written in 673 and which survives in a large number of exemplars.

> É.GAL *šu-a-tú ul-tu* APIN-*šá a-di* GABA-*dib-bi-šá ar-ṣip ú-šak-lil-ma lu-le-e ú-ma-al-li*
>
> that palace from its foundation to its parapet, I constructed, completed and filled it with splendor;

and finally, col. III, lines 12ff with col. VI, lines 10ff of B7:

> ^{d}*A-šur* ^{d}XV *šá* NINA^{ki} DINGIR.MEŠ KUR *Aš+šur*^{ki} *ka-li-šu-nu ina qir-bi-šá aq-ri-ma* UDU.SIZKUR.MEŠ *taš-ri-iḫ-ti eb-bu-ti ma-ḫar-šú-un aq-qí-ma*
>
> Aššur, Issar of Nineveh, all the great gods of the land of Assyria, I invited inside. I made before them extravagant, pure offerings.

Esarhaddon's inscription (B7) which was written in 676, probably would have been familiar to the intended audience of the Naqia inscription.[49] The similarity between the two must have been intentional and served an important purpose which was twofold. On the one hand the correspondence between the two texts emphasized Naqia's important position and her relationship to the king. On the other hand, familiarity with Esarhaddon's text made the differences between the two more noticeable, and these differences served to moderate the image of Naqia that was being presented. Thus for example, while the Naqia inscription contains all the standard parts of a royal building inscription, it does not have any of the common embellishments: the location of the building is given but the exact dimensions and details of engineering are not; we are told that the palace has been filled with splendor but lists of furnishings are left out, for example. Naqia is careful not to overstep the bounds of propriety. Thus, while Esarhaddon invites all the gods of Assyria to the opening of the *ekal māšarti*, Naqia invites only the gods that dwell in Nineveh into her palace. The relationship between Esarhaddon and Naqia is also subtly emphasized. Naqia portrays herself as a loving mother; she mentions her love for her son three or four times. Esarhaddon's support of his mother's project is shown in his donation of men (taken out of his own portion of booty[50]) and his gift of precious material (cypress wood).

---

49 I have argued above (p. 38) that building inscriptions were commonly read aloud at some point during the building of whatever edifice they describe, most probably when it was completed. The fact that the topoi of building inscriptions are well known to us makes Naqia's seem comparable to any number of Sargonid inscriptions, not just Esarhaddons's B7. However, we must remember that, to her audience, the B7 text and the *ekal māšarti* itself were closest in both time and space to Naqia's project, and while I doubt that anyone would have noticed correspondence of exact wording, they almost certainly would have noticed a similarity.

50 An important point which not only shows that he really supports his mother but also reassures that no one else (temples, for instance) got less than their fair share because it went to Naqia. It is possible that the queen mother always got some part of the booty taken on campaign, but this is not certain.

The construction of a palace for the king accomplished several things. It was an unprecedented act which established Naqia as a figure of power. At the same time the building inscription afforded Naqia and Esarhaddon the chance to interpret Naqia's actions for the court, some of whose members might well have considered this act to be patronizing. The inscription was cleverly written to dispel such doubts and to show that Naqia put her son's welfare and comfort first, and that Esarhaddon fully supported the project. We do not know if Esarhaddon ever actually resided there. He built a large residential wing onto the Nineveh arsenal, and it seems likely that he lived there when at Nineveh.[51] Naqia herself, rather than Esarhaddon, may have lived in her palace, which (if true) would also have softened the impact of the project considerably.

Thus the same propaganda methods that the king himself used (manifestations of royal prosperity and power in public works and the textual explanation of these works) were employed to present Naqia as a powerful figure and to explain her status. We can, I think, see a similar use of Esarhaddon's methods in the evidence of Naqia's religious activities. Porter has drawn attention to the fact that theology played a large part in Esarhaddon's presentation of the reconstruction of Babylon to the people of Assyria and Babylonia.[52] Acts of piety – restoration and decoration of temples in Assyria and Babylonia – sent a clear message that Esarhaddon revered the gods of both countries, although the Assyrian gods took precedence.[53] By having Naqia participate in some religious ceremonies and contribute to temples, and by displaying her image in particular sanctuaries, Esarhaddon was able to show that his mother was pious and, by implication, that the gods supported her.[54] There is evidence that Naqia was involved in religious rites and temple administration in no less than five cities: the three main urban centers in Assyria, Assur, Calah and Nineveh; and two important cities in other parts of the empire, Harran and Borsippa. Although as a high-ranking member of the royal family Naqia undoubtedly had religious obligations,[55] we must regard such widespread participation as extraordinary.

---

[51] G. Turner, "Tell Nebi Yūnus: The *ekal māšarti* of Nineveh," *Iraq* 32 (1970): 85.

[52] Porter, *Images*: Chapter six.

[53] Porter, *Images*: Chapters four and five.

[54] I do not wish to suggest that Naqia and Esarhaddon were not genuinely concerned with religious matters – quite the opposite. However, in Assyria, the political and religious spheres were not distinct and there was a close connection between political and religious thought.

[55] It is probable that as queen mother Naqia became responsible for supplying certain temples, as indeed it appears each member of the royal family and some high officials were required to do. See for example, Fales and Postgate, *SAA* VII: part 14, 158-81, "Miscellaneous Temple Offerings,"; and part 15, 182-219, "Offerings for the Aššur Temple." See also their comments, *ibid.*, pp. xxxiv-xxxv, and see below Appendix B, p. 112 and n. 25.

In Assyria, Naqia dedicated cult objects and provided materials for sacred rites. Two dedications survive on a single tablet (*ADD* 645 = *ARU* 14): one side relates a gift of

> *al-gu*-MES *huraṣi šá tam-lit* ^{aban}*surru* ^{aban}[xxx] ^{aban}*samdu* ^{aban}babbar.dil.dil ^{aban}[xxxx] 7½ *mane* 5 *šiqil šuqulti*
>
> a piece of gold jewelry, covered with obsidian, carnelian and *papardillu* stone, weighing 7½ mana, 5 shekels[56]

to Mullissu at her sanctuary in Ešarra at Assur. On the other side is a dedication of

> *irat huraṣi ruššе šá tam-lit aban ni-siq-ti šá* 3 *mane* ¾ MEŠ *šuqultu*
>
> a pectoral of red gold set with precious stones weighing 3¾ mana

to "the Lady" of the Emašmaš temple in Nineveh. Both dedications are made

> *a-na balaṭ Aššur-aḫu-iddina ù ša-a-ša a-na balaṭi-ša arak* [*ume-ša*] *kunnu pale-ša šulmu-ša*
>
> for the life of Esarhaddon and for herself, her own life, the length of her days, the stability of her reign (and) her well-being.[57]

Much has been made of the fact that Naqia used the word *palû* in these inscriptions,[58] although it need be no more than a conventional reference to royal duties.[59] It has also been suggested that the use of different names in the dedications – Zakutu for the Mullissu text and Naqia for the Emašmaš inscription – somehow represents an Assyrian/Babylonian duality,[60] but this seems unlikely in view of the fact that the dedications were made at Assyrian temples. The queen mother's use of the Akkadian Zakutu may simply show the desire to use an Assyrian name when dealing with the consort of the state god. It is probably more significant that the dedications were made to female deities. It may be that the queen/queen mother took a parallel role to that of the king when appealing to female counterparts of male gods.[61]

---

[56] According to *CAD* A I: 338, the word *al-gu*-MES is of "unknown reading and denotes a piece of jewelry."

[57] With slight variation in wording between the two.

[58] See for example, Lewy, *JNES* 11 (1952): 276-77. who takes it to mean that Naqia actually ruled part of the empire for her son. We will discuss this idea in detail in the next chapter.

[59] See below p. 72 for further discussion.

[60] Schmidtke, *AOTU*, I/2: 124: "Es scheint somit, dass sie in Babylonien weiterhin ihren aramäischen Namen führte, während in Assyrien der neue in Gebrauch war."

[61] Reade, *CRRAI* 33 (1986): 143 and Van De Mieroop, *Hallo Fest.*: 259. Both suggest that the inscriptions show a parallelism between the queen and Aššur's consort.

Naqia also donated a necklace to a deity (name not preserved) which was probably worn on its statue.[62]

The inscription on the surviving agate bead is comparable to that of the above dedicatory texts, although much shorter. It reads:

> DIŠ ^{d}[...] ^{MÍ}*za-ku-tú* MÍ.É.GAL *šá* ^{m}30-PAP.MEŠ-SU *šar*$_4$ KUR AŠ DIŠ TI AŠ-PAP-AŠ *šar*$_4$ KUR AŠ DUMU-*šá ù šá-a-šá* DIŠ TI-*šá* BA
>
> To the deity [...] Zakutu, queen of Sennacherib, king of Assyria, for the life of Esarhaddon, king of Assyria, her son, and for herself and her own life, has donated.[63]

There is no way to date any of these dedications but two of them show that Naqia made substantial donations to female deities in different cities. It is probably not coincidental that Esarhaddon did major work at the two temples mentioned in these inscriptions, Ešarra and Emašmaš.[64] Although we cannot necessarily associate the dedications with Esarhaddon's work, we can point out the concurrence of their interests: where Esarhaddon was active, Naqia was also active.

There is ample evidence for Naqia's involvement with the temple of Nabû at Calah, although here again her activities seem limited to the sanctuary of a female deity, in this case Nabû's consort, Tašmetum. Two letters to Naqia regarding the supply of offering materials for the Tašmetum shrine at the Nabû temple seem to indicate that the queen mother had a special relationship to this goddess.[65] *SAA* XIII, 76 and 77 are letters from Nergal-šarrani, a functionary of the Calah Nabû Temple,[66] to the queen mother in answer to her queries:

SAA XIII, 76 obv. 10ff:

> *ina* UGU *ša* AMA.MAN *be-lí iš-pur-an-ni*
> *ma-a mi-i-nu ina* ŠÀ *dul-li il-lak*

---

[62] Van De Mieroop, *Hallo Fest.*: 259-261.

[63] Van De Mieroop, *Hallo Fest.*: 259.

[64] Borger, *Asarh*: 1ff, for the Aššur inscriptions and *ibid.*, p. 66, for Nin G which describes the rebuilding of Emašmaš.

[65] Menzel, *Tempel* I: 296.

[66] The exact office that Nergal-šarrani held is not known, but he must have been a fairly important official since he wrote to the king (*SAA* XIII, 70, 71 and 75) and the queen mother, and dealt with other high officials such as Adad-šumu-uṣur (*SAA* XIII, 71 and *SAA* X, 227). Oates suggests that Nergal-šarrani succeeded Nabû-šumu-iškun as *ḫazanu* of the temple (D. Oates, "Ezida: The Temple of Nabu," *Iraq* 19 [1957]: 35.) and if this is the case it must have happened late in Esarhaddon's reign since, as *ḫazanu* of the temple, Nabû-šumu-iškun writes to the crown prince Ashurbanipal (*SAA* XIII, 78), thus showing he was in office after 672. Nergal-šarrani was the brother of Nabû-nadin-šumi, one of Esarhaddon's exorcists and author of sixteen letters (See *SAA* X, 273-88).

Ì.GIŠ DÙG.GA GAB$^{!}$.LÀL ŠEM.ḪI.(A).MEŠ DÙG.GA.MEŠ
^{ŠEM}ŠEŠ ^{ŠEM}*qu-nu-bu*
[^{ŠEM}]*en*$^{?}$*-du an-ni-ʾu-u*
[*ú*]*-de-e ša dul-li*
[*x x x x am-m*]*ar* AMA.LUGAL
taq-[*bu-u-ni le*]*-pu-uš*
UD.[*x*.KÁM UDU.SISKU]R.MEŠ *šal-ma-a-te*
1-*en* GUD 12 UDU.MEŠ BABBAR.ME
MUŠEN.GAL-*i e-pu-uš*
^{MÍ}*dam*$^{!}$*-qa-a.a* GÉME *ša* AMA.MAN
ina UGU *dul-li la mu-qa-šá*
la te-e-rab
man-nu ša AMA.LUGAL *be-lí*
i-qab-bu-u-ni
qu-up-pu li-ip-te
dul-lu le-e-pu-uš

Concerning what the mother of the king, my lord, wrote: "What is used in the rites?" – Sweet oil, wax (and) aromatic plants... these are the necessary items for the ritual... Whatever the mother of the king ordered, I will surely do. On the xth day I made the correct sacrifices, 1 bull, 12 white sheep (and) a duck. Damqa, the servant of the queen mother cannot take part in the rites. Whomever the mother of the king, my lord, orders, let him open the basket and perform the rite.

and *SAA* XIII, 77 obv. 7ff:

ina UGU UDU.SISKUR.MEŠ *ša iš-pur-u-ni-ni*
ma-a ina IGI *man-ni e-pu-šu*
gab-bu ina IGI ^{d}*taš-me-tum*
in-né-pa-áš
GUD.NITÁ *u* 2 UDU.NITÁ.MEŠ
MUŠEN.GAL-*lum*
PAB *an-ni-ʾu-u šu-u gab-bu*

Concerning the offerings about which they wrote to me, "Before whom do they make them?" – All will be made before Tašmetum. A bull, 2 sheep and a duck – all this is the total.

Parpola considers that both letters refer to daily offerings to be supplied to Tašmetum.[67] Menzel suggests that the letters refer to the twice-yearly *bīt rimki* ceremony for Tašmetum,[68] but it is even possible that they describe

[67] Parpola, *LAS* 2: 300. Compare the lists of items appearing in *SAA* XIII, 77 and 78 with the list in *SAA* VII, 181 obv. 1-2 (Animal offerings from the palace) 1 GUD 10 UDU 1 MUŠEN.GAL KÁ *suk-ki dan-nu* 1 GUD 10 UDU 1 MUŠEN.GAL KÁ *suk-ki qà-li* (one ox, 10 sheep, 1 duck – the gate of the big shrine; 1 ox, 10 sheep, 1 duck – the gate of the small shrine).

[68] Menzel, *Tempel* I: 296.

rituals that were carried out monthly.[69] However, in view of the fact that the queen mother has to ask what to send and which god was involved, it seems more likely that her contributions were made for a special occasion. The rites in question are probably not to be directly associated with the marriage of Nabû and Tašmetum, since the queen mother is never mentioned in the letters concerning this ceremony,[70] but they probably do date to the same general time period.[71]

Not only did Naqia contribute to the Tašmetum sanctuary of the Calah Nabû temple, but according to *SAA* XIII, 61 she was to have her statue made and displayed in that temple.

SAA XIII, 61 is a letter written to Esarhaddon from Urad-Nabû, a functionary of the temple of Nabû at Calah.[72] The letter is a simple report of the receipt of monthly revenue for the temple (here for the month *tašrītu*). However, Urad-Nabû also states that

> KUG.GI *a-na ṣa-lam* LUGAL-*a-ni a-na ṣa-lam ša* AMA MAN *la-a id-din*
>
> he (the palace treasurer) did not give gold for the images of the king and for the image of the king's mother.[73]

Apparently Esarhaddon had commissioned statues of himself and his mother, for which he was supplying at least some of the materials. Since the statues were to be made at the temple, they were probably going to be placed in one of the sanctuaries,[74] in front of, or on either side of the deity's statue as was the custom.[75]

---

[69] Ashurbanipal's hymn to Tašmetum and Nabû (*KAR* 122 = *SAA* III, 6) includes the statement UD-5-KAM ITI-*šam-ma šá-da-aḫ* ^{d}*taš-*[*me-tum* (on the fifth day, monthly, is the procession of Tašmetum). Transliteration and translation from A. Livingstone, *Court Poetry and Literary Miscellanea,* SAA III (Helsinki, 1989): 17.

[70] Several letters were written about this: *SAA* XIII, 56, 70, and 78. For discussion of these letters and the sacred marriage see E. Matsushima, "Le Rituel Hiérogamique de Nabû," *Acta Sumerologica* 9 (1987): 131-75; J.N. Postgate, "The *bit akiti* in Assyrian Nabu Temples," *Sumer* 30 (1974): 51-74; and F. Pomponio, *Nabû – Il culto e la figura di un dio del Pantheon babilonese ed assiro,* Studi Semitici 51 (Rome, 1978).

[71] See p. 44, n. 66 and p. 47, n. 77 for the dating of *SAA* XIII 76 and 77.

[72] Urad-Nabû is the author of at least seven letters in the corpus: *SAA* XIII, 56, 58, 61-65, all of which deal with cultic matters. He is also mentioned in three other letters (*SAA* XIII, 126, 127 and 174) whose contents indicate that he had something to do with the decorations and decorative offerings of the temple.

[73] Rev. 3-5.

[74] The Nabû temple also contained a shrine to Tašmetum, Nabû's consort. See Mallowan, *Nimrud* II: 232 for a plan of the temple.

[75] Note for example *SAA* X, 358, rev. 5ff: *ṣa-lam-a-ni ša* MAN EN-*iá ina* UGU *ki-gal-li i-mit-tú šu-me-le ú-sa-za-a-a-zi* (I set up statues of the king, my lord, right and left on a pedestal) and *SAA* X, 13, rev. 3-5: ⸢*ṣa*⸣-*lam* LUGAL^{MEŠ} KALAG$^{!}$[^{MEŠ}] ZAG *u* KAB ⸢*ša*⸣ ⸢^{d}⸣[30]$^{!}$ *lu-šá-zi-z*[*u*]$^{!}$ (the large statues of the king should be put up on the right and left side of the god [Sin]). For further examples, see *CAD* Ṣ: 81f, and also note Cole's comments in *SAA* XIII: xiii-xv.

It seems likely that Esarhaddon ordered the statues as part of some larger project. Esarhaddon carried out extensive repairs to the Nabû temple at Calah at some point during his reign,[76] and it may be that the statues were commissioned to mark the completion of this project, but this is conjectural. *SAA* XIII, 61, 76 and 77 probably all date to the period 672-669[77] which might indicate that Naqia's contributions were somehow connected to the placing of her statue in the temple.

Naqia is also depicted on the fragment of a bronze relief (Fig. 1, p. 26) which was probably originally part of the facing on the dais/base of a divine throne or an altar.[78] The relief depicts the king, holding a scepter in his left hand, and an object (perhaps an aromatic plant) in his right hand, which he holds up to his nose. The king is followed by the figure of Naqia who holds a mirror in her left hand and the same plant-like object in her right hand, which she also holds up to her nose.

The bronze is inscribed with a text which Parrot and Nougayrol restore as follows:

> [*ina ṣip*]-*pat muš*[*are šá* KAR.ZA.GIN.NA (??)]
> [*pi*(?)-*i*]*ḫ*-*t*[*um*(?)] *š*[*a*(?)] ^{d}*é*[.*a ú-še-reb-ma* (?)]
> [*ina š*]*i-pir apkalli*
> KA.[LUḪ.UD.DA]
> [K]A.DU$_{8}$.Ù[.DA *rim-ki*]
> [*te*]-*lil* [-*te*]
> *ma-ḫar* [*kakkabe*]
> *mu-ši-ti*
> ^{d}[*é.a* ^{d}*Šamaš*]
> ^{d}*asal.lú.*[*ḫi* ^{d}*maḫ*]
> ^{d}*kù.*[*sud*]
> *u* ^{d}[*n*]*in.giri*[*m*]
> *pi-i-šá lu am-si a*[-*na áš-ri* (??)]

---

[76] Mallowan, *Nimrud* I: 239ff and II: 601, identifies Esarhaddon as the king doing the building by the style of construction. Parker, the dig epigrapher, identified two broken prisms found at the temple as Esarhaddon's by comparison to other texts, although the king's name was broken (M.E.L. Mallowan, "The Excavations at Nimrud (Kalḫu), 1955," *Iraq* 18 [1956]: 11).

[77] Datable letters of Nergal-šarrani and Urad-Nabû belong to this period. For example, both authors wrote to the king about the marriage ceremony of Nabû and Tašmetum (*SAA* XIII, 56 and 70, respectively), and mention of the crown princes in *SAA* XIII, 56 makes dating to this period certain. Parpola dates *SAA* XIII, 71 (a letter from Nergal-šarrani to the king regarding fungus on the temple wall) to c. 670 (Parpola, *LAS* 2: 463). Also, it may be that Nergal-šarrani succeeded Nabû-šumu-iškun as *ḫazanu* of the temple (see above p. 4744 n. 66). It seems most likely that these letters, like most of Esarhaddon's letter corpus, date to the last years of his reign.

[78] Parrot and Nougayrol, *Syria* 33 (1956): 147. The measurements of the piece are given in note 2 as: height 33 cm (about 1 foot); width 31 cm (about 1 foot); thickness 15 cm (roughly six inches); and weight 13.9 kg (about 14 kilos or 30 lbs.). For discussion of the attribution of the bronze to Esarhaddon's reign see above Chapter II, pp 25-26.

ṣi-i-ru ki (?) ? ? [...]
[*ina* ^{um}(??) 2]0 (?) $^{\mathrm{K[AM](?)}}$...][79]

[In the orc]hards and ga[rdens of Karzaginna], [I caused a statue? o]f E[a to enter]. Through the knowledge of the experts (I performed) mouth washing, mouth opening, washing and purifying before the stars of night. Ea, Šamaš, Asalluḫi, Maḫ, Kusu and Ningirim, I opened his mouth in an august place ...

This inscription, as it is restored, compares well with a passage in Esarhaddon's text AsBbE[80] in which he describes his major temple restoration projects at Ešarra and Esagila and the return of gods to Babylon:

[79] Parrot and Nougayrol, *Syria* 33 (1956): 153.
[80] And the fragmentary AsBbH (Borger, *Asarh.*: 91, §60).

Fig. 3 *Kudurru* of Marduk-apla-iddina II.
(VA 2663; courtesy Vorderasiatisches Museum, Berlin)

i-na ṣip-pat ^{giš}*kiri palgi mu-šar-e šá É-kar-za-gìn-na áš-ri el-li ina ši-pir apkalli mes pi* (written KA.LUḪ.Ù.DA) *pet pi* (written KA.DU$_8$.Ù.DA) *rim-ki te-lil-te ma-ḫar kak*[*kabe šamami* ^{d}*E-a*] ^{d}*Šá-maš* ^{d}*Asari*(?)*-lú*(?)*-*[*ḫi*] ^{d}*Maḫ* ^{d}*Kù-sù* ...[81]

In the orchards, the canals and gardens of Ekarzaginna, a pure place. Through the knowledge of the experts (I performed) mouth washing, mouth opening, washing and purifying before the stars of heaven. Ea, Šamaš, Asarluḫi, Maḫ, Kusu ...

In view of the similarity between these texts, Parrot and Nougayrol suggest that the Naqia bronze probably belonged on a dais in the Ekarzaginna chapel of Esagila in Babylon, and was put up in the last years of Esarhaddon's reign to commemorate the temple's reconstruction.[82] According to Reade, the gesture of putting the aromatic object up to the nose is one, "of great ritual significance, originating in Babylonia."[83] The subject matter of the inscription, coupled with the Babylonian mannerism rendered in the poses of the figures, might lead us to conclude that the piece was indeed intended for display in Esagila. However, there is reason to believe that the Louvre bronze was displayed in Assyria, rather than in Babylonia.

The artistry of the piece is distinctly Assyrian. According to the letters written by Mar-Issar, the king's official who oversaw the restoration work in Babylonia, the decoration of temples was done locally, although materials were often sent from Assyria.[84] If the Louvre piece had been placed in Esagila, it would have been made in Babylonia by Babylonians and should be recognizably Babylonian in style.

If we compare the Louvre bronze (Fig. 1, p. 26) with the well-known *kudurru* of Marduk-apla-iddina II (Fig. 3), for example, we can see that the bronze is not Babylonian. Note the difference in style between the monuments: the figures on the *kudurru* have soft, rounded forms in contrast to the leaner, more muscled forms of the Assyrian bronze. On the bronze, the king

---

[81] Borger, *Asarh.*: 89, §57, AsBbE r.21-24.

[82] Parrot and Nougayrol, *Syria* 33 (1956):147.

[83] Reade, *CRRAI* 33 (1986): 143.

[84] See for example, *SAA* X, 348 which describes the making of the crown of Nabû. According to the letter it was fashioned in Babylonia, although some material for it was sent from Assyria. See also *SAA* X, 349, 354, 358 and 364, all of which concern the restoration and decoration of Babylonian temples. A notable exception to the rule that temple decoration was done *in situ* is the remaking of the statues of the gods that had been taken to Assyria by Sennacherib. Since they were already in Assyria it was natural (and ideologically necessary) for them to be restored/refashioned there.

is wearing an Assyrian crown and ritual robes (a tiered crown and shawl wrapped diagonally around his body) as distinct from comparable Babylonian garments (smooth crown, pleated robe and wide belt). On the Zinjirli stele (Fig. 4, below), Šamaš-šumu-ukin, crown prince of Babylon, is shown in Babylonian dress very similar to the robes worn by Marduk-apla-iddina on

Fig. 4 The Zinjirli stele; Esarhaddon holds on a leash the king of Tyre and the crown prince of Egypt. At the sides are the Assyrian crown princes Ashurbanipal and Šamaš-šumu-ukin.
(VA 2708; courtesy Vorderasiatisches Museum, Berlin [line drawing after Börker-Klähn, *ABVF*, 219])

Fig. 5 Banquet of Ashurbanipal.
(BM 124920 [detail]; courtesy Trustees of the British Museum)

the *kudurru*. On the Louvre bronze, Esarhaddon is not wearing Babylonian attire.[85] The figure of Naqia is also typically Assyrian: she is almost identical in terms of both style and accoutrements to the figure of Libbali-šarrat as seen on Ashurbanipal's banquet relief (Fig. 5). It is possible that the Louvre bronze was made in Assyria and transported to Babylonia, but this seems unlikely in view of the difficulty involved.

The text AsBbE was discovered in the Aššur temple at Assur,[86] and thus may have been meant for an Assyrian audience.[87] While our text is not

[85] Note for example, *SAA* XIII, 178, a letter to Esarhaddon from Šuma-iddin (who was the *šatammu* of Esagila) in which the writer describes a statue that he has approved and sent on to the king: "you(!) are entering before Marduk, your god; ... the arrangement of the clothing of the king, my lord, is just like that (of the statues) which they are setting up in Assur upon the dais of Bel (and) I have set up in Esaggil and the temples of Babylon" (ll. 10-21). The fact that the *šatammu* of Esagila had to approve the statue's attire suggests that Esarhaddon took care to follow Babylonian customs when it was appropriate.

[86] L. Messerschmidt, *Keilschrifttexte aus Assur historischen Inhalts* I, WVDOG 16 (Lepzig, 1911): XIII.

[87] See Porter, *Images*: Chapter six for discussion of the AsBb texts.

necessarily a duplicate of AsBbE, it may be closely associated. There is also a passage in AsBbE which refers to a cast silver (*ešmaru*) dais decoration in the Aššur temple:

> *ṣa-lam šarru-ti-ia mu-sa-pu-u ilu-ti-šú-un mu-te-riš* [ba]*bálaṭ-iá ù ṣa-lam Aš-šur-bani-apli mar ri-du-ti-ia ab-ta-ni ṣe-ru-uš-šú*
>
> I fashioned upon it (the dais) the image of my majesty in prayer and supplication for my life before their divinity, and an image of Ashurbanipal, my crown prince.[88]

This passage shows that such a dais was an important part of Esarhaddon's Aššur temple decoration, for it showed the king praying before the gods ceaselessly, just as he is depicted on the Louvre bronze. It seems most likely that the bronze was intended for display in a temple in Assyria, probably in one of the chapels of the Aššur temple at Assur.

By commissioning her statue for the temple, and by depicting her next to him on a religious relief, Esarhaddon included Naqia in an area normally reserved for kings. Although it was common for kings to put up statues of themselves, these are the only known instances of a woman's portrait being placed in a temple, at least in Neo-Assyrian times.[89] Naqia's statue and relief portrait represented her status and Esarhaddon's support before the gods and before those Assyrians of high enough rank to gain entrance to the sanctuary.

Naqia also donated to temples in other parts of the empire. *SAA* XIII, 188, a fragmentary letter from a temple official in Harran (name not preserved) to the queen mother[90] describes receipt of donations and work done on one of the temples in Harran:

> *a-na* 30 GÚ.UN [*x*] 6 MA.N[A] KUG.UD
> *a-na-ku* [LÚ]2-*ú ša* [LÚ]EN.NAM

[88] Borger, *Asarh.*, 87, §57, AsBbE r.3ff.

[89] Royal women appear elsewhere in Assyrian art but never in a temple setting. See for example, the stele of Libbali-šarrat, Ashurbanipal's wife, among those from Assur (W. Andrae, *Die Stelenreihen in Assur,* WVDOG 24 (Leipzig, 1913): 7 and Abb. 233; Börker-Klähn, *ABVF*: 227 with further bibliography). For an Old Babylonian example of a statue of a priestess see *UET* 5 75:5.

[90] It is impossible to say for certain that the letter is addressed to the queen mother, since the beginning is so broken. However, the queen mother appears at least six times, making it fairly certain that the letter is addressed to her. The name of the author is not preserved. Parpola (*CT* 53: 14) tentatively attributes the letter to Nabû-zeru-iddina, the son of Urad-Ea and the chief chanter of Ashurbanipal, but the introductory formula does not compare well with those of other letters by Nabû-zeru-iddina (*SAA* X, 345 and 346), but these date to c. 650 (Parpola, *LAS* 2: 371) which might account for the difference. A point in favor of an attribution to Nabû-zeru-iddina is the unusual spelling of Harran in line 5 – [URU]*Ḫar-ra-na* as opposed to the usual [URU]KASKAL. This spelling also appears in the colophon of a text of Nabû-zeru-iddina, *BAK* 500, rev. 8. (Parpola, *LAS* 2: 452). Both Nabû-zeru-iddina and his father Urad-Ea were priests of Sin at the temple in Harran (Parpola, *LAS* 2: 452).

^{LÚ}A.BA ^{LÚ}2-[*ú*] *ša* ^{LÚ}IGI.DUB
^{LÚ}A.BA É.DINGIR ^{LÚ}SANGA.MEŠ
É.DINGIR.MEŠ *ša* ^{URU}*Ḫar-ra-na*
[T]A ^{m}LUGAL-*lu-da-ri* ^{LÚ}*mu-kil*-PA.MEŠ
[*ni-i*]*ḫ-ti-aṭ ni-ta-aḫ-ar*
[*x*] ITI.ZÍZ ŠÀ *x x* ITI.[*x*]
[*x x*]-*ú dul-a-a-n*[*i*]
[*nu*]-*se-li*

30 talents [...], 6 mana of silver, I (and) the deputy of the governor, the deputy scribe of the treasurer, the temple scribe, the priests of the temples of Harran, together with Šarru-lu-dari, the chariot driver, we weighed and inspected (it). (From?) the month Šabattu to the middle of? the month [...] we delivered [...] for the work.

The rest of the letter is too broken for meaningful translation, but apparently describes decoration for the temple and some further work being carried out for the queen mother.[91] It is possible that the temple in question is the Eḫulḫul of Sin at Harran which Esarhaddon restored late in his reign and where the *Akītu* of Sin was celebrated in 670,[92] or some other temple in the vicinity.[93] The high-ranking officials involved in the inspection suggest one of the more important temples in Harran as the subject of the letter. The mention of Šarru-lu-dari, the *mukīl appāte,* also points to a late date for the letter.[94] Although the author of the letter is reporting to the queen mother, we cannot say for certain that she was personally responsible for the donations and the work. If the letter was written concerning the restoration of Eḫulḫul it might have been written to Naqia when Esarhaddon was on campaign in Egypt, but this is conjectural.[95]

The queen mother's involvement in Babylonia has received much attention. Several letters were written to her from Babylonian officials and at least one letter from an Assyrian officer in Babylonia to Esarhaddon mentions the

---

[91] Lines 18-28 mention the tail of a lion (KUN *ša* UR.MAḪ), a bed (GIŠ.NÁ), a doorpost (*sippu*) and a lion (UR.MAḪ) and *dullu eppušu* (doing work). For examples of lion statues as temple decoration see *CAD* N II: 196.

[92] Parpola, *SAA* X, 338 and 343. These are letters written to Esarhaddon from Urad-Ea, the father of Nabû-zeru-iddina.

[93] Note the mention of the town Gadisê (r.18) in broken context. Parpola (and now Cole and Machinist, *SAA* XIII, 188) restores the passage as follows: [*ṣal-m*]*u ša* AMA [LUGA]L *ina* UGU [*x x* M]EŠ *ša*$^{?}$ *ina* ŠÀ SILA$^{?}$.MEŠ ^{URU}*ga-di-*⸢*se-e*⸣ *ú-še-piš* (I had statues of the queen mother put up on the [...] in the streets? of Gadisê). Gadisê was located in the Harran area (see Fales and Postgate, *SAA* XI, 214 l. 7′ and the comments on the Harran census, *ibid*., xxx-xxxiv).

[94] This official is mentioned in *SAA* VII, 5 which is a list of functionaries of the households of the queen mother, the crown prince and the chief eunuch. Parpola dates this text to c. 670 (*LAS* 2: 129). Several of the officials appearing on the list are known to have been active during this period.

[95] However, note the discussion of *SAA* X, 313 below pp. 56-58.

queen mother. Only one of these letters contains any political information at all; the rest are either simple greetings or strictly concerned with religious matters. In the next chapter we shall consider in detail the question of the level of Naqia's involvement in Babylonian administration. Here we wish only to make the point that Naqia involved herself to some extent with the restoration of the country and was particularly concerned with the enactment of rites in at least one temple.

In *SAA* X, 348, Mar-Issar writes to Esarhaddon:

> 26 NA_4 IGI×2^{MEŠ} *ša* NA_4.MUŠ.GÍR *ša* MAN EN-*iá* 1 MA.NA KÙ.GI *ša* AMA LUGAL GAŠAN-*ia* ^{md}PA-ZU ^{LÚ}*qur-bu-tú* ... *na-aṣ-ṣa* ... *ki-i ša* MAN *be-lí iš-pur-an-ni a-na a-ge-e* ^{d}PA *ep-pu-šu*
>
> 26 serpentine beads of the king my lord and one mana of gold of the queen mother my lady, were brought by Nabû-le'i, the bodyguard ... As the king my lord wrote, they will be used for the crown of Nabû.

Parpola dates this letter to 671[96] and notes that the fashioning of the crown of Nabû must be associated with the restoration of Borsippa, "which appears to have begun immediately after Esarhaddon's 2nd Egyptian campaign and continued, simultaneously with the rebuilding of Esangil, at least through the year 670 ...."[97] Here, then, is another case of the queen mother being associated with one of Esarhaddon's projects.

The queen mother evidently kept in touch with the situation in Borsippa by writing to at least one official there. *SAA* X, 154 is a brief letter of greeting and reassurance to the queen mother from Aplâ:

> *a-na* AMA.LUGAL GAŠAN-*iá*
> ARAD-*ka* ^{m}DUMU.UŠ-*a*
> ^{d}EN *u* ^{d}AG *a-na* AMA.LUGAL
> GAŠAN-*iá lik-ru-bu*
> *a-du-ú* UD-*mu-us-su*
> ^{d}AG *u* ^{d}*na-na-a*
> *a-na ba-la-ṭa*
> *nap-šá-a-ti*
> *ù a-ra-ku* UD-*mu*
> *šá* LUGAL KUR.KUR EN-*iá*
> *ù* AMA.LUGAL GAŠAN-*iá*
> *ú-ṣal-la*
> AMA.LUGAL GAŠAN-*a*
> *lu-ú ḫa-ma-ti*
> LÚ.A.*šip-ri šá du-un-qu*
> *šá* ^{d}EN *u* ^{d}AG
> *it-ti* LUGAL KUR.KUR

---

96 Parpola, *LAS* 2: 264.

97 Parpola, *LAS* 2: 63.

be-lí-iá
it-ta-lak

To the mother of the king, my lady, your servant, Aplâ. May Bel and Nabû bless the mother of the king, my lady. Now daily I pray to Nabû and Nanâ for the health, life and length of days of the king of the lands, my lord and the mother of the king, my lady. The mother of the king, my lady, can be confident. The messenger with the favor of Bel and Nabû has gone with the king of the lands, my lord.

The greeting formula of this letter clearly shows that it was written from Borsippa.[98] The author can probably be identified with the astrologer, Aplâ of Borsippa, who sent numerous astrological reports to Esarhaddon's court.[99] Aplâ's statement that "the messenger ... has gone with the king" may be taken literally to mean that he has been sent on to Esarhaddon who must, therefore, have been away from Nineveh. It is also possible to interpret this phrase figuratively as Parpola has in *SAA* X ("a gracious angel of Bel and Nabû has gone with the king ..."),[100] although in either case the implication is that the king is away. It may be that this letter was written to the queen mother when Esarhaddon was away on campaign, and it is possible, albeit unprovable, that the letter was written during Esarhaddon's absence on the Egyptian campaign of 671. A total lunar eclipse occurred while the king was in Egypt[101] which would explain why Aplâ had written to reassure the queen mother.

Naqia also received a letter, *SAA* X, 313, from a Babylonian priest, Nabû-šumu-lišir, concerning the ritual for an eclipse:

a-na AMA.LUGAL EN-*iá*
ARAD-*ka* ^{md}PA-MU-SI.SÁ
^{d}UTU *u* ^{d}AMAR.UTU
šul-mu šá AMA.LUGAL
EN-*iá liš-ʾa-a-lu*
^{mí}*qal-la-ti*
šá ina É ^{m}*Šá-ma-aʾ*

---

[98] For example, Mar-Issar writes about the operation of the cults of Nabû and Nanâ in Borsippa (*SAA* X, 353).

[99] Although according to A.L. Oppenheim, "Divination and Celestial Observation in the Last Assyrian Empire," *Centaurus* 14 (1969): 101, "none of the scholars [Nabû-iqiša, Aplaja and Šapiku] is represented among the writers of the letters to the Assyrian king that were found in the palace at Nineveh in the same archives as the Reports, nor are their names mentioned in these letters." Waterman (*RCAE* III:129); and Streck (*Assurbanipal*: cxl) identify the writer of *SAA* X, 313 with the LÚ.GAL URU.MEŠ *ša* ^{URU}*Laḫiru ša* É AMA.MAN (the chief of towns of Lahiru of the queen mother's estate) of *SAA* VI, 255, but their identification is based on the incorrect reading of the name in this text and must be rejected. For the collated tablet see S. Parpola, "Collations to Neo-Assyrian Legal Texts from Nineveh," *Assur* 2/5 (1979). See also *PNA* 1/I: 116.

[100] Parpola, *SAA* X, 154.

[101] See below p. 58 n. 118.

šá ina pa-ni-iá paq-da-tu
[*x en-n*]*a dul-la*
šá AN.MI *i-ba-áš-šú*
ina UGU-*ḫi-šú*
in-né-ep-pu-uš
AMA.LUGAL *um-ma*
UDU.NITÁ.MEŠ *lid-di-nu*
ki-i pa-ni AMA.LUGAL
mah-ru a-na LÚ.GAL NÍG.ŠID
šá É.GAL
lip-qí-du-ma
UDU.NÍTA.MEŠ *lid-di-nu*

To the mother of the king, my lord, your servant, Nabû-šumu-lišir. May Šamaš and Marduk be concerned with the welfare of the mother of the king, my lord. The female servant who is in the house of Šama', who is in my service – now the rite for the eclipse is ready, it will be performed on her. The mother of the king says "let them give sheep": if it is acceptable to the queen mother let them appoint that the rams be given to the chief of accounts of the palace.[102]

Although Nabû-šumu-lišir does not seem to have written any other letters or astrological reports, he is mentioned in *SAA* X, 371 as ^{d}PA-MU-SI.SÁ DUMU.ŠEŠ-*šu ša Za-ki-ru* ^{lú}*maš-šú-ú* (Nabû-šumu-lišir, the nephew of Zakir, the exorcist).[103] There is little doubt that the Nabû-šumu-lišir mentioned here is the same person as in *SAA* X, 313 because the name is spelled the same way in both cases and both describe the actions of an exorcist.[104] Nothing in *SAA* X, 313, other than the fact that it is written in Babylonian script, helps us identify its point of origin.[105]

Although *SAA* X, 313 deals with the performance of apotropaic rituals concerning an eclipse, it unfortunately contains no astronomical data by which we may identify the specific eclipse. It does not even say whether a

---

[102] This translation is based on Parpola's in *SAA* X.

[103] Note that in *SAA* X, 371 the translation mistakenly says Nabû-zeru-lišir for Nabû-šumu-lišir, although the transliteration is correct (^{d}PA-MU-SI.SÁ) as is the index of names. It is not known whether the uncle of Nabû-šumu-lišir is the same man as Zakir, the prolific writer of astrological reports (*SAA* VIII, 300-315) and at least two letters (*SAA* X, 168 and 169), although this seems likely. Oppenheim (*Centaurus* 14 [1969]:104) says that Zakir wrote from Babylon, but also notes the mention of the Sealand in both *ABL* 137 and 702 (= *SAA* X, 168 and 169), which might suggest that he wrote from further south.

[104] In *SAA* X, 371 (rev. 6-9) Nabû-šumu-lišir is said to have performed the *bīt rimki*, É.GAL.KUR.RA, and *māmēti pašāri* rituals.

[105] Dietrich thinks that *SAA* X, 371 was written somewhere in the territory of Bit-Amukkani (Dietrich, *AOAT* 7: 58). Then, by association, our letter would have been written somewhere in this region, that is the area in southern Mesopotamia including Ur and Uruk (See maps in *AOAT* 7; S. Parpola, *Neo-Assyrian Toponyms,* AOAT 6 [Kevalaer and Neukirchen-Vluyn, 1970]; and in *SAA* I). Dietrich's argument is based on faulty reasoning (for which see J.A. Brinkman, "Notes on Aramaeans and Chaldaeans in

solar or lunar eclipse is meant. Nevertheless, we can draw some valid conclusions from our letter. First of all, we know that since the letter was written from Babylonia, the eclipse in question affected Babylonia, meaning that the eclipse was visible there and darkened the right-hand quadrant of the disc.[106] Now an eclipse affecting Babylonia would only concern an Assyrian king (and his mother) if he ruled in Babylonia as well as Assyria.[107] Prior to 649, while Šamaš-šumu-ukin was king in Babylonia, Ashurbanipal ruled only in Assyria and therefore had no reason to instigate apotropaic rituals in Babylonia after an ominous eclipse.[108] Thus, our letter cannot date to Ashurbanipal's reign, but must deal with an eclipse which occurred during the reign of Esarhaddon.

There were ten lunar eclipses and three solar eclipses visible in Babylonia between the years 680 and 669 BC.[109] Of the ten lunar eclipses, six did not affect Babylonia (July 680, June 679, November 677, February 673, December 670, and June 669) and so need not receive further consideration here.[110] The eclipses of May 678, September 674, July 671 and December 671 were essentially total eclipses.[111] Of the three solar eclipses, the eclipse of June 679 was nearly total and required the enthronement of a substitute king,[112] whereas the eclipses of April 676 and May 669 did not affect Babylonia.[113] We therefore have a choice of five eclipses to which our letter may refer:

Southern Babylonia in the Early Seventh Century B.C.," *OrNS* 46 (1977): 309-12 and 319:29). At present we cannot locate the origin of the letter.

106 For interpretive purposes the disc was divided into quarters, the right hand one of which represented Akkad/Babylonia. Parpola, *LAS* 2: xxiii and appendix F, especially 406-407.

107 Cf. Parpola, *LAS* 2: xxii, "For Esarhaddon, who was king of both Assyria and Babylonia, even eclipses with darkened right-hand quadrant (Akkad/Babylonia) posed a mortal danger." And LAS 2: xxv, "A special case was constituted by eclipses calling for repetition of the enthronement rites [of a substitute king]... For Esarhaddon (and other Assyrian kings who also held the kingship in Babylon), this meant that each time the lunar quadrant corresponding to Babylonia was eclipsed, a substitute had to be placed on the throne in Babylon as well. And if the quadrants of *both* Assyria and Babylonia were eclipsed, as actually happened three times in Esarhaddon's reign, the *same* substitute had to be enthroned in *both* Nineveh *and* Babylon."

108 It is not clear exactly what official relationship existed between Assyria and Babylonia before the Šamaš-šumu-ukin revolt of 652-649 (see Brinkman, *Prelude*: 85ff) but the one case in which Ashurbanipal may have put a substitute king on the throne in Babylonia was apparently a terrible mistake which was quite shocking to Ashurbanipal's advisor (*SAA* X, 89 and 90). "By having a substitute 'sit' in Akkad the king had only been able to assure the safety of the king of Akkad, i.e. Šamaš-šumu-ukin, but had done nothing whatsoever for his own welfare" (Parpola, *LAS* 2: 305).

109 M. Kudlek and E.H. Michler, *Solar and Lunar Eclipses of the Ancient Near East from 3000 B.C. to 0 with Maps,* AOATS 1 (Kevalaer and Neuchircken-Vluyn, 1971): 28 and 146.

110 See Parpola *LAS* 2: 404 (Appendix F) for illustrations of these eclipses.

111 With maximum magnitudes ranging from .94 (July 671) to 1.71 (Sep. 674). Kudlek and Michler, *AOATS* 1:146.

679 (June 17, total solar)
678 (May 22, total lunar)
674 (Sep. 3, total lunar)
671 (July 2, total lunar)
671 (Dec. 27, total lunar)

Four out of these five required the enthronement of a substitute king.[114] The lunar eclipse of May 22, 678 did not call for the enthronement of a substitute king because Jupiter was visible during the eclipse,[115] for this reason we will omit it from further consideration.

SAA X, 313 must have been written concerning an eclipse whose severity called for the enthronement of a substitute king in Babylonia, although it clearly does not deal with the *šar puḫi* ritual itself.[116] In view of the fact that *SAA* X, 371, (the only other document mentioning Nabû-šumu-lišir) refers to the eclipse of July 671 by date, and also to apotropaic rituals carried out by Nabû-šumu-lišir,[117] it seems most likely that our letter deals with the same eclipse, which occurred while Esarhaddon was on campaign in Egypt.[118] Although Esarhaddon's officials obviously had matters well in hand (see *SAA* X, 347), the substitute king was not enthroned in Babylonia until Ululu 4, 671, almost two months after the eclipse.[119] In the interim the queen mother evidently felt that it was necessary to have some apotropaic rituals performed.

We have seen that in Assyria Naqia actively participated in religious matters. Although Naqia's dedications and donations, and Esarhaddon's placing of her statue/image in temples reveal a genuine concern for religious matters, they may also be seen as a concerted effort to put Naqia on the same level as Esarhaddon and to make her appear pious before the gods and before Assyrian court and temple personnel.

---

112 Parpola, *LAS* 2: xxiii.

113 Parpola, *LAS* 2: xxiii; and Kudlek and Michler, *AOATS* 1: 28. Note that the April 676 eclipse was so small (with a maximum magnitude of only .09) that it may not even have been observed.

114 Parpola, *LAS* 2: xxiii.

115 When Jupiter was visible during such an eclipse, the danger to the king was thought to be averted. Parpola, *LAS* 2: xxii.

116 The female servant mentioned in the letter is a stand-in for the queen mother herself who could not be there. As the mother of the king she evidently felt that it was necessary to undergo apotropaic/purification rites whenever ominous events occured, even if they occured in Babylonia.

117 Lines 5f. and rev. 6ff.

118 Esarhaddon's Egyptian campaign apparently began in Nisan and ended in Du'uzu 671. However, it is possible that Esarhaddon was already back in Assyria before the end of the campaign and before the eclipse took place (Parpola, *LAS* 2: 268). Even if this is so, some of his officials in Babylonia evidently did not know of his return to Nineveh, hence *SAA* X, 371 line 5f.: *ul-tu* LUGAL EN *a-na* KUR *mi-ṣir il-lil-lik ina* ITU.ŠU AN.MI *iš-ku-nu* ("after the king, my lord, went to Egypt and an eclipse occurred in the month Du'uzu..." Parpola, *LAS* 2: 64, n.120.).

119 Parpola, *SAA* X, 11, 12, 189 and 314.

Esarhaddon placed his mother's image in two different temples in Assyria sometime during the last years of his reign. At Nineveh Naqia made a dedication to a goddess. At Assur she made a dedication to Mullissu and her image may have been displayed in one of the sanctuaries in Ešarra. At Calah she supplied the Tašmetum sanctuary with offerings and her statue was exhibited in the Nabû temple. In Assyria her religious activities were limited to the worship of female deities. In Babylonia, she had rites performed and donated gold for Nabû's crown. In Harran she contributed to a temple and apparently oversaw at least some of the restoration (perhaps a chapel?). It is no accident that Naqia was active at temples which Esarhaddon also patronized, and it seems likely that Naqia's activities were planned to coincide with his.

We have argued that most of Naqia's religious activities can probably be dated to the period 672-669 of Esarhaddon's reign, and correspond to, not only the mature expression of Esarhaddon's Babylonian policy as it appears in AsBbe (for example),[120] but also with his efforts to establish Ashurbanipal (and to a lesser degree Šamaš-šumu-ukin) firmly as crown prince. During the period 672-669 Esarhaddon had his son's portrait displayed with his own no less than five times. At least two of these were in temples.[121] We find that both Naqia and the crown princes appear or were involved with each of Esarhaddon's important projects during this period. Thus, while Naqia gave gold for the crown of Nabû, Šamaš-šumu-ukin's name was inscribed on the crown alongside Esarhaddon's.[122] Ashurbanipal was depicted in relief next to his father on a metal revetment in the Aššur temple, just as Naqia was shown following Esarhaddon on such a relief. Naqia was closely involved with the Tašmetum sanctuary at the Calah Nabû Temple at the about the same time Esarhaddon and the crown princes prepared for and celebrated the marriage of Nabû and Tašmetum.[123] Esarhaddon restored Eḫulḫul and placed his statue and those of the crown princes in the temple – Naqia sponsored work in the same city, perhaps even the same temple. Although we cannot demonstrate that these activities were carried out simultaneously, we have shown that Naqia was active where Esarhaddon was most active and it seems likely that these instances coincide in time to a degree.

From our investigation it has become apparent that Esarhaddon purposefully set out to present his mother as a figure whose status was almost as high

---

120 The references to Egyptian booty in AsBbE mean that the text must date to 671 or later.

121 An example of both crown princes being placed with the king is *SAA* X, 13, r.6f: *ṣa-lam*^{MEŠ} *ša* DUMU[^{MEŠ}] *ša* LUGAL EN-*ia* ina [...] *ina* IGI ^{d}30 *lu-š*[*á*$^{!}$*-zi-zu*] (the statues of the king my lord's sons should be stood up in front of the moon god). We have already discussed the mention of a dais in the Aššur temple decorated with images of the king and Ashurbanipal (see above p. 52). Esarhaddon also had portraits of the crown princes depicted on the sides of the Zinjirli stele (see Fig. 4, p. 50) and probably at least two other stelae (for which see Börker-Klähn, *ABVF*: 217 and 218).

122 Parpola, *SAA* X, 353: obv. 5-7.

123 *SAA* XIII, 56 and 78.

as the king's. By including her in activities which also promoted the crown princes, Esarhaddon established his mother as a guardian of his heirs. This also explains why he gave his mother such status: he simply wanted someone he could trust to see to it that Ashurbanipal and Šamaš-šumu-ukin took their respective thrones when he died. Having established how and why Naqia was given power, we must now try to determine what form this took in practice. Did the queen mother actually rule any part of the empire? Did she have any political power and if so how is it manifest in the sources? By examining these sources in the broader context of Esarhaddon's reign we should be able to ascertain whether Naqia's power was real or symbolic.

CHAPTER IV

THE POLITICAL STATUS OF THE QUEEN MOTHER

In our study of Naqia as queen mother, we have so far examined her character as it was presented in art and inscriptions to the public and to the gods. We have seen that she was carefully shown as an indomitable, god-fearing woman with strong affection for her son. The media for expressing this message were limited to religious activity and the construction of a palace for the king. Although Esarhaddon's motives for giving his mother a position of authority were political, it remains to be seen whether Naqia actually held a government position, such as a governorship, or whether her position was not so defined.

We shall begin by considering Naqia's position in Babylonia, because the fact that the queen mother received letters from high officials and temple personnel there[1] has given rise to the theory that she actually governed Babylonia for Esarhaddon. However, no one has discussed the sources in detail or made efforts to date them.[2] Only when this is accomplished can we hope to see them in the context of Esarhaddon's reign and thus understand Naqia's role in Babylonia.

According to Esarhaddon's inscriptions, he began the reconstruction of Babylon in his accession year.[3] The work proceeded slowly with a long interval during which it stalled because of lack of funds.[4] Scholars have long speculated about the reasons for Esarhaddon's complete "about face" with respect to his father's Babylonian policy. Sennacherib destroyed the city, laid waste the surrounding countryside and made little or no effort to sustain the economy of the country. Esarhaddon, on the other hand, immediately set about reconstructing Babylon and restoring the social and economic order in the other urban centers. It has sometimes been suggested that Naqia and perhaps Ešarra-ḫamat (Esarhaddon's primary wife) were Babylonian and

---

[1] *SAA* X 154 and 313 were discussed in the previous chapter. *ABL* 254 and 917 are letters to the queen mother from city/district governors.

[2] Dietrich discusses *ABL* 917 and 254 briefly in *AOAT* 7: 26-27 and 53-54, respectively.

[3] Borger, *Asarh.*, 29, §11. Even if this date is fictitious as argued by Landsberger (*BBEA*: 18-20) and more recently by Cogan (*HHI*: 85-87), Esarhaddon is claiming that his intention from the time of his accession was to rebuild Babylon. See also Porter, *Images*: 170-73.

[4] Parpola, *Murderer*: 179-80, n. 41.

therefore influenced him in this matter. As we have seen, however, there is no evidence that Naqia was Babylonian, nor is there proof that Ešarra-ḫamat was.[5]

Esarhaddon's restoration of Babylon and efforts to re-invigorate the entire country were probably motivated by political necessity[6] and divine omens[7] rather than a pro-Babylonian political stance.[8] Both Frame and Porter point out that Esarhaddon's reconstruction of Babylon was a return to the Babylonian policy of his father's predecessors, a policy which Sennacherib himself had implemented until he was driven to abandon it.[9] Although it may not be entirely clear why and how Esarhaddon decided on his Babylonian policy, there is no indication that either his mother or his wife had anything to do with his decision to rebuild Babylon.

Winckler, Lewy and more recently, Dietrich, claim that Naqia actually ruled Babylonia for Esarhaddon during his reign.[10] The evidence for her involvement in Babylonia is restricted. Only one letter written to her from Babylonia touches on political matters (*ABL* 917); the others are religious (*SAA* X, 313) or brief greetings (*ABL* 254 and *SAA* X, 154). Although the latter are terse, we can gain some information from identifying their authors and dating them as exactly as possible. There is only one economic document that contains any reference to the queen mother's presence in Babylonia (*SAA* VI, 255).

From *SAA* VI, 255 we know that in 678 (eponymy of Nergal-šarru-uṣur) Naqia held lands in Lahiru, which may have been the seat of government in Babylonia at the time.[11] The text shows that the queen mother owned an estate there:

---

[5] Above pp. 14-15 and Brinkman, *JAOS* 103 (1983): 36, n. 5.

[6] Porter, *Images*: 29f where she comments, "For eight years until Sennacherib's death Babylonia was quiet, and it appeared that his relentless use of force might at last have ended the long series of Babylonian revolts against Assyrian rule. When Esarhaddon came to the throne after Sennacherib's death, however, it was already apparent that Babylonian resistance had only been lying dormant, recovering strength."

[7] Parpola, *Murderer*: 179, n. 41 "There is no evidence that Esarhaddon ever intended to rebuild Babylon before he received the omen in question; but after it had become publicly known, how could he have adopted any other policy?" According to Esarhaddon's Babylonian inscriptions and *ABL* 1216 the omens (including celestial, liver and lecanomancy) were overwhelming in their agreement that Esarhaddon should rebuild Babylon. He seems to have been cautious – even reluctant – in his acceptance of these signs, only proceeding when a consensus had been reached.

[8] The existence of a pro-Babylonian political party in Assyria has long been suspected, but cannot yet be demonstrated. For more about this topic see Brinkman, *Prelude*: 71 and Grayson, *CAH* III/2: 132-33.

[9] Porter, *Images*: 78; Frame, *Babylonia*: 70.

[10] Winckler *AOF*: 189; Lewy, *JNES* 11 (1952): 272-75 and Dietrich, *AOAT* 7: 26.

[11] Parpola, *LAS* 2: 264 and Lewy, *JNES* 11 (1952): 276. For the location of Lahiru in the Diyala region see J.A. Brinkman, *A Political History of Post-Kassite Babylonia*, Analecta Orientalia, 43 (Rome, 1968): n. 1093.

> [NA$_4$ KIŠ]IB $^{m⌈}$*i*$^{!⌉}$-*du*$^{!}$-*u-a* LÚ.GAL U[RU(.MEŠ)] [*ša* UR]U.*la-ḫi-ra ša* É AMA.MAN
>
> Seal of Idu'a, village manager of Lahiru of the house of the queen mother.

Porter surmises that Naqia may have been "... acting as a provincial governor in the Diyala area."[12] However, owning land, whatever the size of the holding, does not indicate governorship of the surrounding area. There is ample evidence of village managers working for people who were not governors.[13] In any case, one economic document showing that Naqia had an estate at Lahiru early in the reign of Esarhaddon is no indication that she ruled either the Diyala or Babylonia for him.[14]

In *ABL* 917 Na'id-marduk, governor of the Sealand, writes to the queen mother about an Elamite raid on a bridge, presumably somewhere on the border. This is the only letter we have of his, although he is mentioned in several others.[15] It is also the only unequivocal shred of evidence that Naqia was ever involved in Babylonian politics. The letter is not dated, but by placing it in its historical context, we may be able to suggest a date. Esarhaddon ascended the throne in Assyria sometime in Addaru 681.[16] Almost immediately, the situation in Babylonia required his attention: during the confusion after the murder of Sennacherib, Nabû-zer-kitti-lišir, governor of the Sealand and son of Marduk-apla-iddina II, laid siege to Ur, but did not take the city. When Nabû-zer-kitti-lišir learned that Esarhaddon was preparing to send troops to relieve Ur, he fled to Elam with his brother Na'id-Marduk. Nabû-zer-kitti-lišir did not receive the expected Elamite support, and was subsequently executed. Na'id-Marduk then went to Assyria and submitted to Esarhaddon, who appointed him governor of the Sealand.[17]

---

[12] Porter, *Images*: 38, n. 85.

[13] See especially Kwasman and Parpola, *SAA* VI, 60-80, documents of Bahianu, village manager of the temple stewardess (^{MÍ}*láḫ-ḫi-ni-te*).

[14] Another legal document, Kwasman, *NALK* 173, describes a transaction in which Milki-nuri the eunuch of the queen buys land in Lahiru. This can hardly refer to Naqia since the text is dated 671 (it also does not refer to Ešarra-ḫamat since she died in 672, but may mention her successor, perhaps the mother of Šamaš-šumu-ukin?). Robert Whiting has pointed out to me that Kanunaya was also the eponym in 666 and thus the text could refer to the queen of Ashurbanipal, especially since the same Milki-nuri, eunuch of the queen, buys an entirely similar estate in Lahiru in a text dated 668 (*NALK* 174; see above p. 15, n. 18). In any case, the text does not refer to Naqia, but does demonstrate an ongoing royal presence in the area.

[15] *SAA* X, 2 and 327; *ABL* 576, 839, 958, and 1114.

[16] Esarhaddon's annals (Borger, *Asarh.*, 45, §27, Nin A, Ep. 2, 87) give the date of his accession as XII-8, but the Babylonian Chronicle gives the day as 18 or possibly 28 (Grayson, *TCS* 5: 82, iii 38).

[17] Borger, *Asarh.*, 47, §27, Nin A, Ep. 4, 58-64. For discussion of this episode see Brinkman *Prelude*: 72 and Frame, *Babylonia*: 67-68. For a different interpretation of these events see Dietrich, *AOAT* 7: 20-24.

The year Na'id-Marduk took office (680) provides the *terminus post quem* for the letter. We cannot say for certain when Na'id-Marduk left office or under what circumstances he did so. Dietrich argues that he was expelled from office by 675 at the latest and possibly as early as 678, for collusion with one or both of the Babylonian rebels Ṣillaya and Šamaš-ibni.[18] This theory has no solid evidence to back it up and involves a lot of reading between the lines.[19] The fact that Na'id-Marduk is mentioned favorably in Esarhaddon's annals as late as 673 argues strongly against the idea that he was removed from office for treason by 675, and may actually indicate that he still held office at that time.[20] It is possible, however, that (for some reason other than treason) Nabû-eṭir replaced Na'id-Marduk as governor of the Sealand as early as 675.[21] Although we cannot determine the exact dates of Na'id-Marduk's tenure in office, the contents of the letter may allow us to suggest when it was written.

Na'id-Marduk writes to the queen mother as follows:

obv.

a-na AMA.LUGAL *be-lí-ia* ARAD-*ka*
^{m}*na-id-*^{d}AMAR.UTU *lu-ú šul-mu*
a-na AMA.LUGAL *be-lí-ia* AN.ŠÁR ^{d}UTU
ù ^{d}AMAR.UTU LUGAL *be-lí-ia lu-bal-li-ṭu*
ṭu-ub ŠÀ-*bi šá* AMA.LUGAL *be-lí-ia*
liq-bu-ú ul-tu KUR.NIM.MA.KI
a-na UGU-*ḫi-ni il-li-ku-ni-ma gi-iš-ru*
iṣ-ba-tu ki-i šá il-li-ku-ni
a-na AMA.LUGAL *be-lí-iá al-tap-ra en-na*
gi-iš-ru ip-ta-aṭ-ru ù ^{GI}*a-ma-te*
šá gi-iš-ru i-na lu-ka-nu-um-ma
ik-te-lu-ú ul ú-maš-ši-ru-ši-na-ti
ul ni-i-di il-la-ku-ni-i ia-nu-u
ki-i it-tal-ku-ni a-na AMA.LUGAL *be-lí-ia*
a-šap-pa-ra be-lí e-mu-qu liq-[*bu*]*-ú-*[*a*]*n-n*[*a-š*]*i*
DUMU-*šú šá* ^{md}NIN.GAL-SUM-*na a-na* LUGAL KUR.NI[M.MA.KI]

---

18 Dietrich, *AOAT* 7: 33-36 and Parpola *LAS* 2: 37.

19 For a detailed refutation of Dietrich's theory see now Frame, *Babylonia*: 100 n. 178.

20 Borger *Asarh.*, 47, §27, Nin A, Ep. 4, 63-64. The episode about Na'id-Marduk in the Nin A version of Esarhaddon's annals is enlarged and expanded as compared to the earlier version, Nin B7 (for which see Heidel and Oppenheim, *Sumer* 12 [1956]). Tadmor, *HHI*: 46-47 discusses the significance of this change and argues that it was done in order to stress the fate of rebellious vassals (Nabû-zer-kitti-lišir). It is most unlikely that this episode would have been expanded if Na'id-Marduk, who benefits in the story, had subsequently been removed for treason.

21 Frame, *Babylonia*: 89, n. 126. The sequence of governors in the Sealand is not clear. According to Dietrich, Nabû-bel-šumate replaced Na'id-Marduk in the Sealand (*AOAT* 7: 34) in c. 678, but this is based on the incorrect dating and interpretation of *ABL* 839 (on which see Brinkman, *OrNS* 46: 308, n. 27).

⌜*ù*⌝ *a-na* ^m^*ḫu-ma-ni-ga-áš il-ta-p*[*ar x x x x*]
[x x] LUGAL ^KUR^*aš-šur ù ma-dak-ti* [x x x x]

rev.

(beginning broken away)
šu-ú AMA.L[UGAL *be-lí-iá lu-ú i-di*]
ki-i dib-bi ka-a-a-ma-nu-te šú-nu ù
mam-ma i-na ^LÚ^*kal-da-a-nu ap-pit-tim-ma*
il-tap-ra DINGIR.MEŠ *šá* LUGAL *be-lí-iá ki-i*
^LÚ^A.KIN *šá* LUGAL KUR.NIM.MA.KI *ši-pir-e-ti*
la iš-šam-ma a-na pa-ni-iá i-ru-ba ù
a-mu-ru-uš ù mam-ma ši-pir-ta-šú
ip-tu-ú a-di iḫ-ḫi-sú il-li-ku
UD.2.KÁM *šá* ITI.NE ^LÚ^A.KIN-*šú a-na* UGU *mi-iṣ-ru*
a-na pa-ni-iá it-tal-ka a-na ku-tal-li
ul-taḫ-ḫi-is-su ù ^LÚ^A.KIN-*iá*
a-na É.GAL *al-tap-ra be-lí lu-ú*
i-di ki-i ŠÀ-*ba-a it-ti*
É *be-lí-ia gu-um-mu-ru*[22]

To the mother of the king, my lord, your servant Na'id-Marduk. May it be well with the mother of the king, my lord. May Aššur, Šamaš, and Marduk give good health to the king, my lord (and) may they decree happiness for the mother of the king, my lord. They came against us from Elam and seized the bridge. When they came I wrote to the mother of the king, my lord. Now they have taken apart the bridge and they have held back the floats from the bridge. They did not release them. We do not know whether or not they will come (back). If they come I will write to the mother of the king, my lord. May my lord send troops to us! The son of Ningal-iddina has written to the king of Elam and to Ḫumanigaš. [......] and [......]

The mother of the king, my lord, should know that those reports are reliable and someone among the Chaldeans certainly has written. By the gods of the king, my lord! Did a messenger of the king of Elam not bring messages? He came before me and I (swear I) saw him, and (I swear that) no one opened his messages before he returned. On the 2nd of Ab his messenger came to me across the border. I made him go back and I sent my messenger to the palace. May my lord know that my whole heart is with the house of my lord.[23]

---

[22] This transliteration was provided by Simo Parpola and it greatly improves upon the previous transliteration in Waterman, *RCAE*: 917.

[23] In general the letter is well preserved but it contains a number of obscure passages. For a different transliteration and translation of parts of this letter see Dietrich, *AOAT* 7: 144-45.

The letter describes an Elamite raid on the Sealand and includes a request that troops be sent in case hostilities continue. Na'id-Marduk also mentions that a son of Ningal-iddina (the governor of Ur) has written to the king of Elam; presumably he regards this as an act of disloyalty during a time of friction between the two countries.[24] In general, however, relations between Elam and Assyria were cordial during the reign of Esarhaddon, so it is probable that *ABL* 917 should be associated with one of the known incidents of hostility. We know for instance, that Nabû-ušallim, another son of Marduk-apla-iddina, made an attempt to gain control of the Sealand from his brother. According to *ABL* 576 and 1114,[25] he had Elamite backing, which would suggest that the attempt occurred before Ḫumban-ḫaltaš II's death in 675, for his successor, Urtak, maintained good relations with Esarhaddon.[26] In fact the only military action between the two countries that can be dated with certainty occurred in 675 when, according to the Babylonian chronicle, the Elamites made a raid on Sippar.[27] This may well have been timed to coincide with Nabû-ušallim's effort to gain control of the Sealand.[28]

There is no firm way to connect *ABL* 917 with Nabû-ušallim's coup attempt and it should be noted that we do not even know how far this insurrection went (whether any violence actually occurred). However, *ABL* 917 would fit well in the context of *ABL* 576 and 1114 in which the Elamites claim suzerainty over the Sealand through Nabû-ušallim. Such a predicament would certainly have inspired Na'id-Marduk to ask for troops (*ABL* 917, obv. 15: may my lord send troops) and to stress his continuing loyalty to Assyria (rev. 13-15: May my lord know that my whole heart is with the house of my lord). The writers of *ABL* 1114 say they have written about the situation more than once, apparently with no response from Assyria, rev. 23-24:

---

[24] The letter is broken here and it is difficult to interpret the context in which Ningal-iddina's son is mentioned. For a different interpretation see Dietrich, *AOAT* 7: 26-27.

[25] *ABL* 1114, obv. 14-19 and 576 obv. 7-14. It should be noted that Dietrich, *AOAT* 7: 24-25 argues that these letters date to the period immediately following Nabû-zer-kitti-lišir's death (680) when Na'id-Marduk was in Assyria, and that Porter, *Images*: 35, n. 75, follows Dietrich. However, it seems unlikely that the Elamites would first put Nabû-zer-kitti-lišir to death in apparent support of the Assyrians and then instantly reverse their policy. It makes more sense to associate the Elamite attempt to oust Na'id-Marduk with later events.

[26] For detailed discussion of Assyrian-Elamite relations during the reign of Esarhaddon see Brinkman *Prelude*: 78-79; Frame, *Babylonia*: 82-83 and 88-89; and J.A. Brinkman, "The Elamite-Babylonian frontier in the Neo-Elamite Period, 750-625 B.C.," in De Meyer et al. eds. *Fragmenta historiae elamicae: mélanges offerts à M.-J. Stève* (Paris, 1986): 199-207.

[27] Grayson, *TCS* 5: 83, iv 9.

[28] 675 also saw troubles arise in Nippur and Bit-dakkuri, although it is by no means certain that the Elamites took advantage of this. For a discussion of these events see Brinkman *Prelude*: 76 and 78 and Frame, *Babylonia*: 82-89.

ù am-me-ni I-*šu* II-*šu a-na šarri be-lí-í-ni ni-iš-pu-ram-*[*ma*]

and why have we written to the king, our lord, once, twice?

Na'id-Marduk, too, claims to have written to the queen mother earlier (obv. 8-9: when they came I wrote to the mother of the king), without receiving any response. It therefore seems most likely that *ABL* 917 dates to c. 675.

If the people of the Sealand were having difficulty convincing Esarhaddon that the situation was serious, Na'id-Marduk might well have turned to the queen mother, assuming that if he could get her support she might be able to prompt Esarhaddon into action. Na'id-Marduk could have made her acquaintance when he was at the Assyrian court in 680, and, since Esarhaddon's annals tell us that he returned to Assyria with tribute annually,[29] it would have been easy for him to remain in close contact with the queen mother. Lines 3ff of the reverse (The reports are reliable and someone among the Chaldeans certainly has written) seem to be in direct response to a letter from Naqia. There is a tacit understanding that he was writing all the news at her request (thus the references to previous and future letters: I wrote when they came, I will write if they come again). Still, Na'id-Marduk need not have been writing to Naqia as his official superior and there is nothing in the letter that would support such a conclusion.

There are, of course, other ways to explain why Na'id-Marduk wrote to the queen mother. Dietrich argues that since *ABL* 917 is the only letter from Na'id-Marduk in the corpus, he obviously reported to someone other than the king, i.e. Naqia at Lahiru.[30] However, Dietrich is arguing *ex silentio* and until there is some real proof of this suppostition it is best keep a simpler explanation for Na'id-Marduk's action. We should also point out, *contra* Dietrich, that no letters from provincial governors have been preserved in the correspondence of Esarhaddon, and therefore the absence of Na'id-Marduk's letters is not exceptional.[31] The simplest explanation for Na'id-Marduk having written to the queen mother is that he knew her to be influential and needed someone to draw his problem to the king's attention. There is no evidence that he was required to report to Naqia or that she held an official position as his superior.

A second problematic letter from Babylonia is *ABL* 254, a short greeting to the mother of the king from Ašaredu:

a-na AMA.LUGAL
be-lí-iá
ARAD-*ka* ^{m}*a-ša-re-du*
^{d}AG *u* ^{d}AMAR.UTU
a-na AMA.LUGAL

---

[29] See above, p. 64 n. 20.

[30] Dietrich, *AOAT* 7: 6. Dietrich also assumes that Nabû-bel-šumate (whom he wrongly names as Na'id-Marduk's successor) also reported to Naqia (37, n. 2).

[31] Parpola, *ARINH*: 122.

be-lí-iá lik-ru-bu
UD-*mu-us-su*
^{d}U.GUR *u* ^{d}*la-aṣ*
a-na DIN ZI.MEŠ
šá LUGAL *u* AMA.LUGAL
be-lí-MEŠ
ú-ṣal-lu
DI-*mu a-na* URU
u É.DINGIR.MEŠ
šá LUGAL *u a-du-u*
ma-aṣ-ṣar-tú
šá LUGAL *be-lí-iá*
a-na-aṣ-ṣar[32]

To the mother of the king, my lord, your servant Ašaredu. May Nabû and Marduk bless the mother of the king, my lord. Daily I pray to Nergal and Laṣ for the life and welfare of the king and the mother of the king, my lord. It is well with the city and the temples of the king, and now I am keeping the watch of the king, my lord.

Several people with the name Ašaredu are known to have been active in Babylonia during this period: the astrologers Ašaredu *pānû*[33] and Ašaredu *qatnu;*[34] the author of *ABL* 254, *SAA* X, 155, 156 and *CT* 54, 538; and the *šākin ṭēmi* of Cutha.[35] *CT* 54, 538 is broken and the author's name is not preserved, but the fact that the greeting formula contains the same unusual sequence of gods (Nabû, Marduk, Nergal and Laṣ) – albeit also partially broken – as in *ABL* 254, suggests that the author is the same.[36] Although neither *SAA* X, 155 nor 156 contains the Nergal and Laṣ greeting, they are generally accepted, presumably on orthographic grounds, to be by the same author as *ABL* 254. The cult center of Nergal and Laṣ was Cutha and their appearance in the greeting formula of our letter indicates that it was written there.[37] Now the basic question of attribution is this: can the author of the letters be identified with either the governor of Cutha or one of the astrologers, or is it possible that a single man wrote letters and reports, and at some point held the office of governor?

There is some confusion in the sources as to just when Ašaredu was governor of Cutha. Dietrich supposes that he held office during the first half

---

[32] This transliteration was provided by Simo Parpola.

[33] Hunger, *SAA* VIII, 336-55.

[34] Hunger, *SAA* VIII, 323-35.

[35] Mentioned in *SAA* X, 163, 7-11 and 164, 8ff. Frame suggests that Nergal-ašarid may be identical with Ašaredu who governed the city during Šamaš-šumu-ukin's reign (Frame, *Babylonia*: 233 and 273). See also *PNA* 1/I: 140-41 for all the prosopographical information.

[36] Dietrich, *AOAT* 7: 53 n.1 and *WO* 4: 219 n. 69.

[37] *RLA* L: 506 and Dietrich *WO* 4: 219 n.69.

of Esarhaddon's reign and was denounced and removed from office as part of the Sasiya conspiracy by c. 675.[38] However, this hypothesis mainly rests on Dietrich's interpretation and restoration of *ABL* 1345 in which Ašaredu's name is not fully preserved and in which his connection to Sasiya is not clear.[39] There really is no evidence that Ašaredu was removed from office and no solid proof that he even held that office during Esarhaddon's reign.[40] On the contrary, an economic text from Cutha[41] shows that Ašaredu was *šākin ṭēmi* of the city in 656, which could mean that he had been re-instated by Šamaš-šumu-ukin, had never been removed from office, or had not held the office until Šamaš-šumu-ukin's reign.[42] Although it is likely that the author of *ABL* 254 who did, after all, write from Cutha, can be identified with the governor of Cutha, there is no reason to insist that he wrote the letter *when* he was governor. The author of the letter was probably one of the astrologers of that name who may have also held the office of governor. The consensus is that Ašaredu *qatnu* wrote from Babylon, so we may conclude that the author of *ABL* 254 was probably Ašaredu *pānû*.[43] This astrologer was active during the whole of Esarhaddon's reign and at least the early years of Ashurbanipal's reign.[44]

Although *ABL* 254 is a short letter consisting only of a greeting formula, an assurance that all is well and the statement that the author is doing his job, it is in some respects ambiguous. For example, from lines reverse 2-4 (it is well with the city and the temples of the king) one might assume that the letter was written by the governor of the city.[45] However the next statement (and

---

[38] Dietrich, *AOAT* 7: 53f and *SAA* X, 163 and 164 for Nabû-iqbi's letters of denunciation. Dietrich identifies Nabû-iqbi with the astrologer of the same name, which is probably correct, since he is known to have written from Cutha. However, note that the datable reports of this astrologer (Hunger, *SAA* VIII, 416-19) are all from Ashurbanipal's reign.

[39] Dietrich, *AOAT* 7: 162. Dietrich restores *ABL* 1345 from the following fragments: K 1919, 7378, 12958, 13081, 15416 and 16116. See *CT* 53, 37 for a copy of the restored tablet.

[40] Complaints were made against Ašaredu of Cutha but we cannot date them securely. See above note 38.

[41] J.A. Brinkman and D.A. Kennedy, "Documentary Evidence for the Economic Base of Early Neo-Babylonian Society: A Survey of Dated Babylonian Economic Texts, 721-626," *JCS* 35 (1983): K.51 and Frame, *Babylonia*: 273, n.30.

[42] It is also possible that the late reference is to a different Ašaredu altogether.

[43] Note, however, that Oppenheim thinks Ašaredu *pānû* also wrote from Babylon (*Centaurus* 14: n. 27).

[44] Hunger, *SAA* VIII, 323 dates to either 680 or 668; 324 and 325 date to 675; 326 dates to 670; 327 dates to 669; and 328 dates to 667.

[45] Compare for example G.B. Lanfranchi and S. Parpola, *SAA* V, 15, a letter from the governor of Amidi to Sargon II, obv.4-5: DI-*mu ana* KUR *ša* LUGAL DI-*mu ana* HAL.ṢU.MEŠ (It is well with the country of the king, it is well with the forts); or S. Parpola, *SAA* I, 31, a letter from Sennacherib to Sargon II, obv. 4-6: *šul-mu a-na* KUR.*aš-šur*.KI, *šul-mu a-na* É.KUR.MEŠ-*te*, *šul-mu a-na* URU.*bi-rat ša* LUGAL *gab-bu* (The country is well, the temples are well, all the king's forts are well).

now I am keeping the watch of the king) is definitely in keeping with the letter of a scholar.[46] If we were to accept the hypothesis that Ašaredu wrote to Naqia when he was governor of Cutha, it might perhaps add a certain credence to the theory that she was ruling Babylonia: this would be the second letter to her from a provincial/city governor. However, the letter itself is devoid of political information; its sole purpose is to report that things are running smoothly. This need not indicate that Ašaredu wrote to Naqia as his immediate superior, but would fit well with the idea that Naqia became especially concerned with Babylonia when Esarhaddon was on campaign or ill. In that case it would be natural for the governor of Cutha, or one of the officials whose duty it was to report omens to the king, to assure her that the situation in the city was stable.

The other two letters written to the queen mother from Babylonian officials (*SAA* X, 154 and 313) and the letter from Mar-Issar to the king in which Naqia is mentioned (*SAA* X, 348), were discussed in the previous chapter. However, we should recall that *SAA* X, 154 was written when the king was away from Assyria,[47] just as *SAA* X, 313 was probably written while the king was in Egypt.[48] It seems likely that the letters written to Naqia from Babylonian officials (with the exception of *ABL* 917) were written when the king was away on campaign, and reveal Naqia's concern for the continued stability of the situation in Babylonia, rather than her direct involvement in the government there.

As we have seen, there is very little evidence for Naqia's involvement in Babylonia. The letters that were written to her from Babylonian officials do not, with the exception of *ABL* 917, contain any political information at all. *ABL* 917 was probably a special case, and the fact that this letter was found in the archive at Nineveh indicates that Naqia, far from taking action in the matter, simply passed the letter along to the proper authorities (which is basically what the letter asks her to do, in any case).[49] The other three letters simply contain greetings and assurances. That they were put in the palace archives suggests that they were not part of a larger correspondence.

Although it is possible that Naqia was in charge of the administration of Babylonia at some point during Esarhaddon's reign, the existing sources do not seem to support such a conclusion. We must also ask what possible advantage her governorship would have held for Esarhaddon? If, as we proposed in the preceeding chapter, Esarhaddon promoted the image of his mother as an authority figure in order to secure the throne, it seems likely that

---

[46] See for example, Hunger, *SAA* VIII, 386, an observation of Rašil, rev. 10-11: *ú-zu-za-ku-ma* [EN.NUN *šá* LUGAL *be*]*-lí-ia a-na-ṣa-ri* (I am standing here and I am keeping the watch of the king, my lord) and 296, observation of Nabû-iqiša rev.7: *ma-aṣ-ṣar-ti šá* LUGAL *be-lí-iá a-nam-ṣar* (I am keeping the watch of the king, my lord). See also Parpola, *SAA* X: xix-xxiv for the significance of "the watch of the king."

[47] See above, p. 55.

[48] See above, pp. 56-58.

[49] Obv. 14: (may my lord send troops!). Note Dietrich gets around this by assuming that the masculine *bēlī* actually refers to Naqia.

he would have kept her close by in order to achieve this end. Evidence suggests that Esarhaddon himself took a strong interest and an active role in governing Babylonia.[50] His whole public relations policy involved presenting himself as a real Babylonian king. Putting his mother as governor over the Babylonians during this period would hardly have advanced his case. Additionally, Mar-Issar, Esarhaddon's envoy at large in Babylonia who oversaw the reconstruction, wrote regularly to the king but never to the queen mother.

Naqia was undoubtedly interested in the political situation in Babylonia, but the evidence of the three letters (*ABL* 254, *SAA* X, 154 and 313) and the letter from Mar-Issar to the king (*SAA* X, 348) suggests that her only means of action there was through religious activity. She had rituals enacted in certain locations (the area of Bit-amukkani(?), perhaps Borsippa and Cutha) and contributed to the restoration of the temple at Borsippa (at least to the statue of Nabû). We cannot say if she did these things on a regular basis or only at times of specific need, because we cannot securely date any of the letters (except *SAA* X, 348). We do not know whether they belong to a short period of time during Esarhaddon's reign, which might indicate, for example, that they were all written at the time of the ominous eclipse of 671, or if they can be spread throughout his reign, thus representing her continued interest. It seems most likely that three of the letters (*ABL* 254, *SAA* X, 154 and 313) date to the period when Esarhaddon was away on campaign in Egypt. We do not wish to suggest that Naqia was left to govern while Esarhaddon was absent, however. On the contrary, the letters reflect the concern of someone who wields no executive authority.

The evidence tends to suggest that Naqia was simply worried about the situation in Babylonia. Rather than attribute her concern to a pro-Babylonian political stance (or even national feelings), it seems most likely that Naqia was apprehensive lest Babylonia become for Esarhaddon the major political and military quagmire it had been for Sennacherib.[51] She would have been well aware of the "evil omens" that appeared in Babylonia during Sennacherib's reign,[52] of the reports that his advisors there did not keep the king informed,[53] and, of course, of the continuous, difficult military involvement in the area. Sennacherib spent his entire reign trying to find a way to rule Babylonia. His efforts were frustrating, costly and tragic (he lost his son). The memory of all of this must have influenced both Naqia and Esarhaddon. However, there is no reason to believe that Naqia held any position in Babylonia other than that of a concerned and influential queen mother.

Naqia's political position in Assyria is much more difficult to ascertain than her position in Babylonia, because the Assyrian sources concerning her are uniformly mute about politics. This silence in itself may be significant

---

50 Porter, *Images*: 79.

51 See for example, J.A. Brinkman, "Sennacherib's Babylonian Problem: An Interpretation," *JCS* 25 (1973): 89-95.

52 Hunger, *SAA* VIII, 502, r.13-18.

53 *SAA* X, 109, r.1-10.

and probably indicates that she did not hold a formal office. Nevertheless, the existing sources may reveal something about the queen mother's status.

In the last chapter we studied the text *ARU* 14 only in the context of temple dedications. We noted, however, Naqia's use of the word *palû* (rule, reign) in two dedications: "for the life of Esarhaddon and for herself, her own life, the stability of her reign and her well being".[54] Some scholars have taken this reference to her rule literally and believe it must mean that she ruled a part of the empire.[55] It does not necessarily follow, however, that Naqia would only use the word *palû* if she was actually ruling a part of the empire or controlling a large administrative unit within it. *ARU* 17, a dedication made by Libbali-šarrat contains similar wording:[56]

> [*a-na balaṭ*] *ᵐaššur-bani-apli na-ra*[*m*]-*i-ša* [*u la*]-*bar ⁱˢᵘkussi-šu ša-a-ša a-na balaṭ-ša arak ume*ᵐᵉˢ-*ša kun-nu pal-e-ša* ...
>
> for the life of Ashurbanipal, her beloved, and for the durability of his throne and for herself, for her own life, length of days and stability of her reign.

There is no evidence that Libbali-šarrat ever ruled any part of the empire, and it seems most likely that the word's appearance in such texts represents a scribal convention.

In addition to the above, letters provide our only other means of assessing Naqia's position in the realm, for she is not mentioned in the royal inscriptions or chronicles of the period. The administrative and economic documents that refer to Naqia (see Appendices A and B) do not have any bearing on our evaluation of Naqia's political status.

We have previously analyzed letters written to Naqia from Assyrian temple personnel (*SAA* XIII, 61, 76, 77, and 188). Aside from those letters, there are only three fragmentary letters to the queen mother from Assyrian officials (*SAA* X, 16, 17 and *CT* 53, 182), and one letter to her from the king himself (*ABL* 303). In addition, there is a group of letters written to the king from his exorcists and physicians regarding the health of the queen mother, and one letter to Ashurbanipal in which Naqia is mentioned (*SAA* XIII, 154). There are no surviving letters from the queen mother. With the exception of *ABL*

---

[54] For the transliteration, see above, p. 43.

[55] For example, Lewy, *JNES* 11: 273.

[56] Although the text does not mention the queen by name or title, it seems likely that she made the dedication. Streck, *Assurbanipal*: 392 restores *ummu* ᵐᵈ*aššur-ban-aplu* (mother of Ashurbanipal). Grayson cites this passage in Streck in *CAH* III/2: 139 when he says that the mother of Ashurbanipal was alive when he reigned (his argument depends on whether one thinks Ešarra-ḫamat was Ashurbanipal's mother or not; this question is not within the scope of the present discussion, however). Given the fact that in line 4 it says *narāmiša* (her beloved) rather than the expected *māri narāmiša* (her beloved son) it is most likely that the text was written by Ashurbanipal's queen.

303, we can date the above letters to the period 672-669,[57] the period during which Esarhaddon was most active in establishing the image of his mother as family protector/authority figure. Therefore we may expect them to reflect the success or failure of the king's message, even if they do not tell us outright whether or not the queen mother formally held office.

The letters from Assyrian court personnel to Naqia are unfortunately in extremely fragmentary condition. Only a few fragmentary lines survive of *CT* 53, 182 and they do not reveal anything about the queen mother's status. *SAA* X, 16, a letter from Issar-šumu-ereš, is the best preserved of these letters and the only one where the sender's name has survived. Parpola suggests that *SAA* X, 17, which he also attributes to Issar-šumu-ereš, may actually be part of *SAA* X, 16.[58] We will therefore translate them as one, while retaining their separate numbers:

LAS 21 = *SAA* X, 16:

obv.

a-na AMA LUGAL [EN-*ia*]
ARAD-*ki* [I]15-MU-[KAM-*eš*]
lu DI-*mu a-na* AMA LUGAL EN-*ia*
[d]PA *u* [d]AMAR.UD
a-na AMA LUGAL EN-*ia*
lik-ru-[*bu*]
[...] ⌈[d]AMAR⌉.[UTU]
(the rest of the obverse is broken)

rev.

(beginning lost)

LAS 230 = *SAA* X, 17:

[*ki*]-*i ša* DINGIR[MEŠ] *ga-mir*
[*b*]*é-et ta-kar-ri-bi-ni*
ka-ri-ib
É *ta-na-zi-ri-ni*
na-zi-ir
ina UGU *ša* AMA L[UGAL]
[*b*]*e-li iš-pur-an-*[*ni*]

---

57 Argumentation for dating of the *SAA* X letters is given in *LAS* sub these letters (*SAA* X, 16 = *LAS* 21; *SAA* X, 17 = *LAS* 230; *SAA* X, 200 and 201 = *LAS* 159 and 160; *SAA* X, 197 = *LAS* 222). *SAA* XIII, 154 is written to the crown prince and therefore also dates to this period.

58 Parpola, *LAS* 2: 27 and 220.

[*ma*]-⌜*a*⌝ *mì*-⌜*i-nu*⌝ *x* [...]
(remainder lost)

LAS 21 = *SAA* X, 16

rev. (cont.)

lu-ú [...]
dNIN.LÍL x[...]
lu-ú ta-⌜*qi*⌝-[*iš*]
UDMEŠ GÍDMEŠ DÙG.G[A ŠÀ-*bi*]
ḪÚL ŠÀ-*bi x* [...]
a-na LUGAL ⌜*a*⌝-[*na* DUMU.LUGAL]
a-na MU ⌜*šá*⌝ [AMA LUGAL?]
lu-ú ta-d[*in*]!

(*SAA* X, 16) To the mother of the king, my lord, your servant Issar-šumu-ereš. May it be well with the mother of the king my lord. May Nabû and Marduk bless the mother of the king, my lord ... Marduk ... (*SAA* X, 17) [The verdict of the mother of the king, my lord] is as final as the gods.' What you bless is blessed; what you curse is cursed. Regarding what the mother of the king, my lord wrote to me ... (*SAA* X, 16) May Mullissu grant [...] (and) give long-lasting days, happiness (and) joy [...] to the king, [the crown prince] and the name [of the mother of the king].[59]

Issar-šumu-ereš was the chief scribe of both Esarhaddon and Ashurbanipal and the author of seventy-two letters and astrological reports to these kings.[60] According to Parpola, Issar-šumu-ereš's career lasted from c. 682-650.[61] If line 6 of the reverse of *SAA* X, 16 is restored correctly ("to the king, [the crown prince] and the name [of the mother of the king]") then the letters must date to the period 672-669. However, Parpola, apparently rejecting his own restoration, claims the fact that these are, "the *only* letters to the queen mother in the present corpus suggests that they were written in an exceptional situation, possibly immediately after the death of Esarhaddon (early Nov. 669 BC) when Naqia temporarily held the reins of the empire."[62] At present we see no reason to date the letters to the period following Esarhaddon's death, and prefer to leave the dating open within the period 672-669.

Regardless of their dates, *SAA* X, 16 and 17 do reveal a certain amount about how Naqia was treated by one of Esarhaddon's top advisors. The

---

59 The transliterations are from *SAA* X. The translations are my own, although they closely follow Parpola's (note especially *SAA* X, 17 where he restores "the verdict of the mother of the king, my lord").

60 Parpola, *LAS* 2: XV and for the letters *SAA* X, 5-38. For the astrological reports see now Hunger, *SAA* VIII, 1-38.

61 Parpola, *LAS* 2: 468.

62 Parpola, *LAS* 2: 27.

solicitous tone of *SAA* X, 16, coupled with the comment in 17 about the effectiveness of the queen mother's curse, which is otherwise said only of kings,[63] indicates that Issar-šumu-ereš approached the queen mother as he would the king or crown prince, with due respect and deference. Judging from the letter(s) of Issar-šumu-ereš, Esarhaddon's efforts to establish his mother as an authority figure were successful.

The letters from Esarhaddon's chief exorcists (Adad-šumu-uṣur and Marduk-šakin-šumi) and physician (Urad-Nanâ) concerning Naqia's illness of June 670[64] are generally professional and do not reveal their authors' opinions of the queen mother. However, *LAS* 184 = *SAA* X, 244 (Marduk-šakin-šumi to the king) includes the comment, MÍAMA LUGAL [*k*]*i*!-*i a-da-pi* [*t*]*a*!-*la-*ʾ*i-i* (the mother of the king is capable as Adapa), which, like the remark in *SAA* X, 16, is also used only to characterize kings.[65] Here again we see Naqia elevated to the level of the king and given an unusual measure of respect. It would seem safe to conclude that at least among Esarhaddon's "inner circle"[66] of advisors, Naqia was accepted as a powerful and influential person.

SAA XIII, 154 is a letter to the crown prince, Ashurbanipal,[67] from Dadî, son of Bel-remanni, and priest of the temple of Issar Bit-Kidmurri,[68] complaining of an injustice done to him:

LÚGAL.⌈*da*!-*ni*!⌉-*ba*!-*te* [69]
ša la LUGAL
ša la DUMU LUGAL
i-ṣab-ta ú-sa-ni-qa-a-ni
É.AD-*ia*
*in-ta-áš-*ʾ*a*
a-mar ša AD-*u-a*
ṣil-li LUGAL
iq-nu-u-ni
*in-ta-áš-*ʾ*a*
i-ta-ši

---

63 Parpola, *LAS* 2: 231.

64 For discussion of her illness see Parpola *LAS* 2 sub these letters and below Chapter V.

65 Parpola, *LAS* 2: 176.

66 For the use of this phrase to describe the officials closest to the king see Parpola, *LAS* 2: vx-xxi and Parpola, *SAA* X: xxv-xxvii.

67 It should be noted that both A.L. Oppenheim, *Letters From Mesopotamia* (Chicago: University of Chicago Press, 1967): 182 and Waterman, *RCAE* I: 103 tentatively identify the crown prince as Esarhaddon, although there is nothing in the letter to support this. Since we have no letters from the time that Esarhaddon was crown prince, but we do have many from the period 672-669, it seems much more likely that the letter was sent to Ashurbanipal.

68 Located in Calah (Menzel, *Tempel*: 102-103).

69 Note that Menzel, *Tempel*: 103, Oppenheim, *Letters*: 182 and Waterman, *RCAE* I: 104, read this as the *rab qaqulate*. I follow the transliteration given to me by Simo Parpola.

1 GÚ.UN MA.NA KUG.UD
ba-áš-lu
20 MA.NA KUG.UD
ša a-nu-ut É
na-mu-ra-a-te ša LUGAL
ša AMA LUGAL
i-se-niš i-ta-ši

The chief victualler has seized me and imprisoned me without the (knowledge) of the king or the crown prince (and) he has plundered my father's house. Whatever my fathers have acquired under the shadow of the king, he has plundered and taken away. One talent of silver and twenty pounds of silver in household utensils, gifts given (to my father) by the king (and) the king's mother he also took.

There are several points of interest in this letter. First, we note that Dadî accuses the chief victualler of having carried out these actions against him without permission from the king or the crown prince. It is perhaps safest to assume that the particular chief victualler involved was a member of the crown prince's household, otherwise we must consider that the letter has far-reaching implications concerning the joint-rule of the king and the crown prince. In any case, it is not the queen mother's authority that has been flouted. However, by mentioning that his father had the patronage of both the king and the queen mother, Dadî attempts to strengthen his case. Bel-remanni must have been an important official for he is said to have received the gifts "in the shadow of the king," a phrase which denotes special privileges.[70] Although we do not know why Bel-remanni was given gifts or over what period of time he received them, they provide further evidence of Esarhaddon and Naqia acting in conjunction.

We might expect a letter from the king to his mother to be most revealing about her position in the kingdom. *ABL* 303, our only letter from Esarhaddon to Naqia, is not explicitly informative, however.[71] The letter is as follows:

a-bat LUGAL *a-na*
[MÍ]AMA.MAN
DI-*mu a-a-ši*
lu DI-*mu a-na*
[MÍ]AMA.MAN
ina UGU ARAD *ša* [m]*a-mu-še*
ša taš-pur-in-ni
ki ša [MÍ]AMA.MAN
taq-bu-u-ni
a-na-ku ina pi-it-te-ma

[70] A.L. Oppenheim, "Assyriological Gleanings IV," *BASOR* 107 (1947): 9.

[71] There is no concrete evidence in *ABL* 303 to prove that Esarhaddon sent it, although I know of no one who holds a contrary view.

aq-ṭi-bi
SIG$_5$ *a-dan-niš*
ki-i ša taq-bi-ni
a-na mì-i-ni
^{m}*ḫa-mu-na-a-a*
il-la-ak[72]

Word of the king to the mother of the king. I am well. May it be well with the mother of the king. Concerning the servant of Amuše about whom you wrote. – Just as the queen mother ordered, I have ordered. What you told me is very good. Why should Ḫamunaia come?

Although the letter does not contain any revelations about the queen mother's status, the abbreviated style and lack of explanation indicate that the king and his mother communicated regularly. In this instance, the king was influenced by his mother. It is important to note, however, that Naqia did not have executive power: she could not implement her decision, the king had to give the orders. We cannot infer from such a brief letter that Naqia influenced Esarhaddon in matters of state at all. On the contrary, it would seem that even on mundane matters Naqia had to ask the king to act for her. Although *ABL* 303 suggests that Naqia had access to the king who responded positively to her wishes, it does not lead one to conclude that the queen mother held a formal government post of any kind.

In this chapter we have investigated the actual status of the queen mother. We have analyzed the sources for her presence in Babylonia and Assyria and we have seen that in no instance can it be demonstrated that she ruled any part of the empire, held an administrative position, or influenced Esarhaddon in political matters. On the other hand, we have seen that high officials in both Assyria and Babylonia treated her with respect and deference, sometimes even elevating her (in a figurative way) to the level of the king. We may conclude two things from this: first, the king's efforts to present the queen mother as an important personality were accepted by officials at his court and in Babylonia; second, the king's program did not include giving Naqia a formal position.

---

[72] This transliteration was provided by Simo Parpola.

CHAPTER V

THE ZAKUTU TREATY AS THE CULMINATION OF NAQIA'S POLITICAL CAREER

Having come to the throne after a brief but hard-won civil war, Esarhaddon was particularly concerned about the threat of rebellion, and because his own accession had been so difficult, he was determined to pass the throne to his heirs without the eruption of strife. As part of his response to these problems, Esarhaddon worked with his mother to develop her public image as a person of regal stature whose strength of character could sustain the throne in times of need and see to it that Esarhaddon's heirs took their rightful places after he died. The efforts of the king and queen mother to do this, which were largely carried out during the last four years of Esarhaddon's reign, were effective, and Naqia was accepted as a powerful and influential person at court. In this chapter we will discuss how Naqia fulfilled her designated role when she was called upon to do so.

The years 672-669 mark the realization and fruition of many of Esarhaddon's aims and policies: Esarhaddon designated his heirs, conquered Egypt, and saw his restoration of Babylon reach its final stages. Yet this time was also fraught with political stresses and frustrations, and periods of ill health. Each of Esarhaddon's accomplishments carried its own political price. In designating his heirs, Esarhaddon not only passed over the eldest son in favor of a younger son, but he also arranged for the eventual division of the empire between the two.[1] This unprecedented act caused astonishment and possibly controversy in Assyria.[2] We may infer that the move caused some controversy from the fact that Esarhaddon included such elaborate, lenghty stipulations in the Succession Treaty of 672.[3] The conquest of Egypt in 671[4] allowed

---

[1] Esarhaddon's intentions in this matter are not clear, but he probably meant for Babylonia to be subordinate to Assyria. See among others, Porter, *Images*: 133ff; Parpola *LAS* 2: 116; Frame, *Babylonia*: 95ff.

[2] See Parpola, *SAA* X, 185 = *LAS* 29, the famous letter to Esarhaddon from Adad-šumu-uṣur regarding the naming of the crown princes: *ša ina* AN-*e la e-piš-u-ni* LUGAL *be-lí ina kaq-qi-ri e-tap-áš* (what has not been done in heaven, the king my lord has done on earth ...). See also Parpola's discussion of this letter in *LAS* 2: 116.

[3] D.J. Wiseman, "The Vassal-Treaties of Esarhaddon," *Iraq* 20 (1958): 1-100; and for the most recent edition, Parpola and Watanabe, *SAA* II, 6.

[4] Grayson, *TCS* 5: Chronicle I, iv, 23-28; and Parpola, *SAA* X, 371: 5ff.

Esarhaddon to divert some of the booty taken on the campaign to refinance the flagging restoration work in Babylonia.[5] The level of expenditure required for the rebuilding in general may not have been viewed favorably in Assyria.[6] In addition, the king's health deteriorated steadily during this period.[7]

In Nisan/March 670 an insurrection started in the Harran area.[8] That it became very serious is evident from the entry in the Babylonian Chronicle:

> MU 11.KÁM LUGAL (*ina*) KUR *aš+šur* ^{LÚ}GAL^{MEŠ}-*šú ma-du-tú ina* ^{GIŠ}TUKUL *id-dak*
>
> In the 11th year, the king (in) Assyria executed many of his magnates.[9]

According to Parpola, the rebellion may have taken several months to quell, "... considering the graveness of the crime and the severity with which it was punished, it seems certain that the conspirators did not capitulate instantly but offered strong resistance ...."[10] The severity of this *coup d'état* is also manifest in a group of queries whose purpose was to discover whether or not an anticipated appointee to office could be trusted.[11] Starr suggests that the

---

5 Esarhaddon gave booty for temple reconstruction in Babylon, Borsippa, Nippur and Uruk (Borger, *Asarh.*, 94, §64, Smlt: 28-29; and Brinkman, *Prelude*: 75 n. 368 for further references).

6 Although the existence of pro- and anti-Babylonian parties in Assyrian political circles has yet to be proven (Brinkman, *Prelude*: 71), it seems certain that Esarhaddon's Babylonian policy caused some controversy in Assyria. The fashioning and return of the statue of Marduk seem to have been particularly delicate topics which required special handling for Assyrian audiences (See Porter, *Images*: 143-47 and Frame, *Babylonia*: 71-72.). In the recent edition of the so-called 'Sin of Sargon' text, Parpola argues that the text dates to 671 or 670 and is designed to convince the Assyrians that the making of Marduk's statue, and, by association, the restoration of Babylon, was done at the behest of his father (Sennacherib) and of the gods (H. Tadmor, B. Landsberger and S. Parpola, "The Sin of Sargon and Sennacherib's Last Will," *SAAB* 3 [1989]: 47; for other editions of this text see H. Tadmor, "The 'Sin of Sargon,'" *Eretz Israel* 5 [1958]: 93* [English summary] and 150-63 [in Hebrew]; and Livingstone, *SAA* III, 33). The AsBb texts (Borger, *Asarh.*: 78-93) and possibly the 'Ordeal of Marduk' text were also designed to show that Esarhaddon was acting at the bidding of the gods. (T. Frymer-Kensky, "The Tribulations of Marduk: the so-called 'Marduk Ordeal Text,'" *JAOS* 103 [1983]: 132). Note however that previous interpretations of this text considered it to be anti-Babylonian, probably dating to the reign of Sennacherib (W. von Soden, "Gibt es ein Zeugnis dafür, daß die Babylonier an die Wiederauferstehung Marduks geglaubt haben?" *ZA* 51 [1954]: 130-66; *idem*, "Ein neues Bruchstück des assyrischen Komentars zum Mardukordal," *ZA* 52 [1955]: 224-34; Landsberger, *BBEA*: 15f, n. 9; and Th. Jacobsen, *Treasures of Darkness: A History of Mesopotamian Religion* [New Haven and London: Yale University Press, 1976]: 232).

7 Parpola, *LAS* 2: 235.

8 Parpola, *LAS* 2: 239 n. 418 for the starting location of the revolt. See Larsen, *RA* 68 (1974): 22 for the starting date (Nisan, 670).

9 Grayson, *TCS* 5: Chronicle I, iv, 29.

10 Parpola, *LAS* 2: 239-40.

11 Starr, *SAA* IV, 150-80.

executions carried out as a result of the rebellion, "may account for the numerous vacancies open to prospective aspirants to office whose loyalty was being tested by means of divination."[12] If this is indeed the case, then it is especially interesting that *SAA* IV, 151 regards the appointment of a bodyguard for Naqia. It is possible that someone in her household was among those who conspired to overthrow Esarhaddon.

Open rebellion – the thing Esarhaddon had feared for so long – had finally come to pass. The stresses of the insurrection may have proved too much for the king's health and in Iyyar/May 670[13] (when the revolt had probably not been completely extinguished) he suffered an acute attack of the disease that periodically plagued him.[14] Nine or more letters in Esarhaddon's letter corpus refer to this episode (*SAA* X, 43, 295, 296, 241, 242, 243, 315, 316, 325).[15] It is apparent from these texts that the king nearly died as a result of his illness.[16]

We do not know what role Naqia played during this crisis, but it is possible that the letters *SAA* X, 16 and 17 date to this period, rather than to the weeks following the king's death as suggested by Parpola.[17] It is likely that the queen mother was on hand from the first word of trouble, and it would have been appropriate (according to their preparations) if Naqia had exercised her authority when Esarhaddon fell ill.[18] Under these circumstances Issar-šumu-ereš' comment about the efficacy of the queen mother's curse (*SAA* X, 17 rev. 1-5) – a compliment normally only paid to kings – does not seem so unusual. She may have played an important part in the government at the time.

In any case, Esarhaddon and Naqia survived the emergency. The king recovered from his illness, the *coup d'état* was thwarted, the court and

---

[12] Starr, *SAA* IV: lxiii.

[13] See Parpola, *LAS* 2: 229-30, and sub the letters listed below for the dating rationale.

[14] Parpola identifies it as systemic lupus erythimatosis, a chronic and incurable disease of the central nervous system (*LAS* 2: 230-34). Note, however, Roth's reservations about the identity of Esarhaddon's disease (review of Parpola, *LAS* 2, *ZA* 75 (1985): 309, n. 3). The previous bout of illness (for which we have evidence) occured shortly after the appointment of Esarhaddon's heirs in 672 (Parpola, *SAA* X, 355 = *LAS* 282 and Hunger, *SAA* VIII, 1).

[15] = *LAS* 51, 130, 143, 180, 181, 183, 246, 247, 248.

[16] See for example *SAA* X, 242 = *LAS* 180, 5-10: *ša* LUGAL *be-lí iq-bu-ni ma-a a-hi-ia še-pi-ia la-mu-qa-aia ù ma-a* IGI-*ia la a-pat-ti ma-a mar-ṭak kar-rak ina* ŠÀ *ša ḫu-un-ṭu* (What the king my lord said: "My arms (and) my legs are weak and I cannot open my eyes. I am sick and I lie prostrate"); and *SAA* X, 315 = *LAS* 246, 7-10: *ka-aia-ma-nu* LUGAL *be-lí i-qab-bi-ia ma-a a-ta-a ši-ki-in* GIG-*ia an-ni-u la ta-mar bul-ṭe-e-šú la te-pa-áš* (The king, my lord, keeps saying, "why don't you recognize the nature of this illness of mine and make a remedy for it?"). Note also the myriad therapies and ritual cures listed in these letters that were used in an effort to cure the king.

[17] See above, pp. 74-75 for a translation and discussion of these letters.

[18] Ashurbanipal would have played an important role as well. *SAA* X, 195 = *LAS* 130, a letter to the crown prince from Adad-šumu-uṣur, may date to this period. Note also *ABL* 1257 to Esarhaddon from Ashurbanipal possibly concerning the rebellion (see Parpola, *LAS* 2: 240 and n. 422).

administration were altered accordingly, and security was restored.[19] However, as the severity of the crisis dissipated, in Du'uzu/June 670, the queen mother became seriously ill.[20] Four of Esarhaddon's top advisors were called upon to cure the queen mother. They reported their progress to the king in a series of four letters: *SAA* X, 200 and 201 from the exorcist Adad-šumu-uṣur; *SAA* X, 244 from the exorcist Marduk-šakin-šumi;[21] and *SAA* X, 297 from the exorcist Nabû-šumu-uṣur and the physician Urad-Nanâ together.

The letters were written over a short period of time – a few days to a couple of weeks[22] – and are easily placed in chronological order. The first letter is *SAA* X, 200, written when the queen mother was ill:

> ^{MÍ}AMA LUGAL EN-*ia* DINGIR^{MEŠ} GAL^{MEŠ} *šul-mu a-dan-niš a-dan-niš liš-ku-nu* ... U[Š$_{12}^{!}$].⌜BÚR⌝.RU.DA^{MEŠ} SIG$_{5}^{\text{MEŠ}}$ *ma-a'-du-ti né-ep-pa-áš lib-bu šá* LUGAL EN-*iá lu-u* DÙG.GA
>
> (May the great gods give very very good health to the mother of the king, my lord ... We are performing many good counterspells. The king, my lord can be happy).[23]

Next is the second letter by Adad-šumu-uṣur, *SAA* X, 201, which describes the rituals she has performed and assures the king that his mother's condition is improving:

> ^{MÍ}AMA LUGAL *a-d*[*an*$^{!}$-*niš*] *a-dan-niš šu*[*l-mu*] *l*[*ib-b*]*u šá* LUGAL [EN-*ia a-dan-niš a*]-*dan-niš* [*lu-u* DÙG.GA]

---

[19] Not until Tašritu/October was the vacancy in Naqia's household filled (Starr, *SAA* IV, 151). It was also in this month that Esarhaddon required officials in Babylonia to swear an oath of loyalty (*SAA* X, 254 and Landsberger, *BBEA*).

[20] Parpola dates these letters to Du'uzu/June, 670 on the basis of the sequence of Adad-šumu-uṣur's letters to Esarhaddon concerning the condition of the king (see *LAS* 2: 138 for the list of pertinent letters) and other patients mentioned (charge of *Šarrat Parṣi* and the queen mother). Thus in Ajaru/April, 670 the king is well but the charge of *Šarrat Parṣi* is ill (*LAS* 151 = *SAA* X, 194); by Simanu/May the king's condition is serious and the charge of *Šarrat Parṣi* is still sick (*LAS* 143 and 123 = *SAA* X, 196 and 197); and by Du'uzu/June the king's health has improved but the queen mother is ill (*LAS* 159 and 160 = *SAA* X, 200 and 201).

[21] Two other letters by this exorcist (*LAS* 186 and 187 = *SAA* X, 245 and 246) may refer to rituals (probably of the *maqlu* or *šurpu* type) performed by the queen mother, although she is not mentioned by name in either letter. Parpola dates these letters to June/July 670 and it seems likely that (if these letters do refer to Naqia) that the rituals described had to do with her illness. See comments *LAS* 2: 180-83.

[22] See above n. 20.

[23] Obv. 4-9 and rev. 6-10. It is not certain that the lines about the *ušburruda*s actually refer to the queen mother, although this would make the most sense. See Parpola's comments, *LAS* 2: 147.

Reverse:

(beginning lost)
[ÉN ^{d}É]-*a* ^{d}UTU ^{d}[ASAR.LÚ.ḪI] *ša ma-mit pa-š*[*á*$^{!}$*-a-ri*]
ÉN *at-ti* Í[D$^{!}$ DÙ-*at ka-la-ma*] 10 *ṭup-pa-an-ni a-d*[*i* ...]
te-ta-pa-áš [*šul-mu*] *a-dan-niš lib-bu šá*
LUG[AL EN-*ia*] *a-dan-niš lu-u* DÙG.[GA]

The mother of the king, my lord is doing very very well. The king, my lord can be very very happy.

The incantation "Ea, Šamaš, Asalluhi" of (the ritual) "breaking the curse"; the incantation "You, River, Creator of Everything": she has performed ten tablets until [...] (and) is very well. The king, my lord can be very happy.[24]

The other two letters in the group (*SAA* X, 297 and 244) both state that the queen mother has recovered:

[*šul*]-*mu a-dan-niš a-na* ^{MÍ}AMA LUGAL [*šum*]-*ma šir-ir-šá* [*la i-ṭi-b*]*u*$^{!}$-*ši-ni*

The mother of the king is doing very well. Verily she has recovered.[25]

The severity of Naqia's illness is further indicated by the fact that at least one query to Šamaš was made in an attempt to find out whether she would recover at all:

^{MÍ}*ni-iq-a* AMA ^{md}*aš-šur*-ŠEŠ-SUM-*na* LUGAL ^{KUR}*aš-šur*.KI *šá i-na-an-na mar-ṣa-tu-ma* ŠU ^{d}DUG$_{4}$-*bi*-SIG$_{5}$ *i-na* MÁŠ *iš-šá-ak-un-ši*

Niq'a, mother of Esarhaddon, king of Assyria, who is now ill, and on whom the 'hand' of Iqbi-dammiq was placed in extispicy.[26]

---

[24] The translation is Parpola's with minor differences.

[25] *SAA* X, 297, obv. 9-11. *SAA* X, 244 is almost identical:[*a-dan*]-*niš* [*šul-mu a*]-*na* ^{MÍ}AMA LUGAL [EN-*ia* UZ]U$^{!}$-*šá* DÙG.GA-*ši* (The mother of the king my lord is doing very well. She has recovered). Translation is Parpola's from *SAA* X.

[26] Starr, *SAA* IV, 190 obv. 2-3. Numbers 191, 192 and 193, all of which are similar, may also refer to Naqia, although no name is preserved. Starr tentatively restores Naqia's name in 191, but he does not do so in 192 and 193. Number 195, which is also similar, is definitely not related to Naqia's illness because it is dated to the month Arahsamma (November).

Iqbi-dammiq does not appear in any of the other medical queries or in the diagnostic literature,[27] although this god is named in *Šurpu,*[28] which suggests that the query may have concerned a specific illness.

Without a detailed description of the symptoms Naqia suffered, it is difficult to determine the nature of her illness. The incantations and rituals that Adad-šumu-uṣur and his colleagues used to treat the queen mother provide the only clues about the identity of her ailment. In *SAA* X, 200 Adad-šumu-uṣur comments on the performance of *ušburruda*s on the queen mother's behalf, that is rituals and incantations against witchcraft and sorcery. The ritual *māmīt pašāri* (breaking the curse) mentioned in *SAA* X, 201 was used to cure diseases thought to have been brought on by curses.[29] The incantation *Atti* ÍD is a component of various *namburbi* rituals,[30] the most relevant of which is a *namburbi* against sorcery:

> [NAM.BÚR.BI ḪUL *kiš-pe-e ru-he-e ru-se-e up-š*]*a-še-e* ḪUL.MEŠ *šá* LÚ MÍ *il*ˈ*-pu-tu-ma*
>
> Namburbi for the evil of sorcery, witchcraft, magic (and) evil spells which affect a man (or) woman.[31]

The evidence is unanimous in indicating that the exorcists and their physician colleague diagnosed Naqia as the victim of a witch or sorcerer's curse. In addition, the fact that three exorcists and only one physician applied their expertise to the case is in keeping with the treatment of an illness caused by witchcraft.[32]

According to Parpola, the incantations and rituals used to cure Naqia suggest that the queen mother was suffering from psychological rather than purely physical disorders.[33] This theory is in agreement with the arguments presented by Kinnier Wilson in his article, "An Introduction to Babylonian Psychiatry."[34] In particular, Kinnier Wilson argues that the series *ušburruda*

---

27 For *Enūma ana bīt marṣi* see R. Labat, *Traité akkadien de diagnostics et pronostics médicaux* (Leiden, 1951).

28 E. Reiner, *Šurpu. A Collection of Sumerian and Akkadian Incantations,* AfO Beiheft 11 (1958) tablet II, 158.

29 *CAD* M I: 192-94 for references to *māmīt pašāri* = dispelling of a curse.

30 See Parpola, *LAS* 2: 148 for a list of these *namburbi*s and add R. Caplice, "Namburbi texts in the British Museum," *OrNS* 39 (1970): 148, l. 5.

31 Caplice, *OrNS* 39: 134-41.

32 Some *ušburruda*s contained recipes for treating bewitched patients with drugs, salves and potions and were used by physicians (*asutu*). See references in J.V. Kinnier Wilson, "An introduction to Babylonian psychiatry," *Studies in Honor of Benno Landsberger on his Seventy-fifth Birthday, AS* 16 (Chicago, 1965): 296, n. 19, and additions in Parpola, *LAS* 2: 147.

33 Parpola, *LAS* 2: 148 and 215.

34 Kinnier Wilson, "Psychiatry" *AS* 16: 289-98.

describes psychoses[35] and that the word *māmītu*, specifically as it appears in *Šurpu*, denotes a condition of obsessive/compulsive behavior which may include both a compulsion to do something (i.e., steal, cheat, lie, ...) or a phobia against doing something (paranoia).[36] In our case, the incantations and rituals are consistent with each other; they all are used to treat witchcraft-induced illnesses. At present we cannot say for certain that Naqia's illness was a psychological disorder, but in view of the circumstances preceeding its onset, this seems a most likely conclusion. When the stresses Naqia experienced in the few weeks before her illness had been removed, the queen mother experienced a short period of severe reaction. In technical terms Naqia suffered an episode of "brief reactive psychosis," which typically occurs after a period of intense stress.[37]

Interesting as theories about ancient psychiatry may be, it is impossible to establish an exact correlation between the modern clinical diagnoses of psychiatric disorders and the various incantations and ritual series of ancient Assyria. We must exercise caution when inferring the origins of an illness solely from the treatment prescribed. Whether or not the nature of the queen mother's illness was psychological, physiological or a mixture of the two, cannot be determined with certainty.

What is significant about Naqia's malady is that her recovery was considered to be of great importance. The time and effort expended on curing the queen mother cannot merely be ascribed to a son's concern about his mother. No matter how he felt about her, it was politically important to Esarhaddon that Naqia recover. Consider the situation in the summer of 670. When the king became deathly ill during a period of political upheaval, Naqia almost certainly prepared to act swiftly to put Ashurbanipal on the throne in case Esarhaddon died. She may even have taken a hand in the government when Esarhaddon was sick. Yet Esarhaddon came back from the brink of disaster: he recovered his health and the stability of his throne only to have his mother – his "insurance" against future disaster – fall seriously ill. Quite simply, her death would have ruined all their plans, so every effort was made to make her well.

Naqia and Esarhaddon were not mistaken in thinking the king's death was at hand. Just over a year after the events discussed above, Esarhaddon fell ill on his way to Egypt and died on Arahsamma 10 (November 1), 669.[38] Ashurbanipal was crowned king some twenty days later on Kislev 1 (Novem-

---

[35] Kinnier Wilson, "Psychiatry" *AS* 16: 296. References to the series UŠ$_{12}$.BÚR.RU.DA are given on page 296 n. 19. See also Parpola's comments and further references given in *LAS* 2: 147.

[36] Kinnier Wilson, "Psychiatry," *AS* 16: 294f.

[37] The definition of brief reactive psychosis is given in R.P. Halgin and S.K. Whitbourne, *Abnormal Psychology: the human experience of psychological disorders* (Fort Worth, Harcourt Brace Jovanovich, 1993): 454: "a disorder characterized by the sudden onset of psychotic symptoms that are limited to a period less than a month, and which develops in response to a stressful event or set of events."

[38] Grayson, *TCS* 5: Chronicle I, iv, 30-31.

ber 22).[39] During the interval between Esarhaddon's death and Ashurbanipal's coronation, the queen dowager, Naqia, imposed a loyalty oath (the so-called Zakutu treaty) on behalf of her grandson, Ashurbanipal.[40] The treaty marks the fulfillment of Naqia's mission: she saw to it that the rightful heir took the throne. This is the end of Naqia's involvement in affairs of state. There is no evidence that she took any part in political, administrative or religious events after this date.[41]

The Zakutu treaty is a unique document — the only Assyrian treaty in existence to have been imposed by someone other than the king.[42] Yet it is not surprising that Naqia carried out her duty by imposing an oath: Esarhaddon himself required his subjects and vassals to swear loyalty no less than three times during his reign.[43] Esarhaddon apparently relied on such oaths to help restore order after times of crisis. It seems most likely, therefore, that Esarhaddon and Naqia actually *planned* for her to impose a loyalty oath on behalf of the new king.

The Zakutu treaty only makes sense when put in its proper context. When viewed by itself the treaty suggests either that the queen mother was inordinately influential, as Grayson supposes,[44] or that the political situation at the time required some exceptional act to safeguard the throne, as Tadmor

---

[39] Parpola, *LAS* 2: 430.

[40] L. Waterman, "Some Koyunjik Letters and Related Texts," *AJSL* 29 (1912): 1-36; S. Parpola, "Neo-Assyrian Treaties from the Royal Archives of Nineveh," *JCS* 39 (1987): 167-68 and Parpola and Watanabe, *SAA* II, 8. Note that Wiseman, *VTE*: 9 surmises that the treaty may date to the beginning of the Šamaš-šumu-ukin revolt in 652. This is hardly likely however, since Šamaš-šumu-ukin is a party to the treaty and is not referred to as king.

[41] In fact the only hint we have that she lived after 669 is the economic document *SAA* VI, 325 which may refer to the mother of the king and is dated 663: NA4.KIŠIB m*as-qu*!*-di* LÙ.A.BA ⸢*ša* AMA!⸣ [MAN] (seal of Asqudu, scribe of the [queen] mother). If Ashurbanipal's mother was Ešarra-ḫamat who died in 672 then we know this text refers to Naqia. Parpola regards it as certain that Ešarra-ḫamat was Ashurbanipal's mother (Parpola, *LAS* 2: 120 and 195 and *JCS* 39: 168 n. 24), but Grayson (*CAH* III/2: 139), among others, does not hold this view. We need not be bothered by the fact that *SAA* VI, 325 refers to the mother of the king rather than the grandmother, because Naqia calls herself the mother of the king in the Zakutu treaty. Due to the poor preservation of the text and the doubt about who Ashurbanipal's mother was, we cannot say for certain that it refers to Naqia.

[42] For other Assyrian treaties see Parpola and Watanabe, *SAA* II.

[43] In 680, shortly after he seized the throne, Esarhaddon imposed an oath, a copy of which survives in *SAA* II, 4 (see also Parpola, *JCS* 39: 170-74). In 672 he imposed a loyalty oath on behalf of Ashurbanipal, the so-called "vassal-treaties" (Parpola and Watanabe, *SAA* II, 6; Wiseman, *VTE* [1958]; K. Watanabe, *Die* adê-*Vereidigung anlässlich der Thronfolgeregelung Asarhaddons,* BaM Bh 3 [Berlin, 1987]). In 670, after the *coup* attempt, he imposed yet another loyalty oath on officials in Assyria and Babylonia (Parpola and Watanabe, *SAA* II, 7 and Parpola, *JCS* 39: 174f).

[44] Note for example Grayson's comment that the treaty is "evidence that her influence increased even farther with the accession of her grandson." (*CAH* III/2: 140).

proposes.[45] In order to understand the treaty in its proper perspective, we must quote it in full here:[46]

The Zakutu Treaty = *ABL* 1239 + *JCS* 39, 189

^{1}[*a-d*]*e-e* ⸢*šá*⸣ MÍ.*za-ku-u-te* MÍ.KUR *šá* ^{m}30-P[AB$^{!}$.MEŠ-SU]
^{2}[MA]N KUR-*aš* AMA ^{m}*aš-šur*-PAB-AŠ MAN KUR-*aš-šur*
^{3}TA ^{md}GIŠ.ŠIR-MU-G[I].NA PAB *ta-li-me-šú*
^{4}TA ^{md}GIŠ.ŠIR-UG$_{5}$.GA-TI.LA *ù*
^{5}*re-eh-te* PAB.MEŠ-*šú* TA NUMUN LUGAL TA
^{6}LÚ.GAL.MEŠ LÚ.NAM.MEŠ LÚ.*šá-ziq*$^{!}$*-ni*
^{7}[L]Ú.SAG.MEŠ LÚ.GUB-IGI TA LÚ.⸢*zak*⸣*-ke-e*
^{8}*ù* LÚ.TU-KUR *gab-bu* 0$^{!}$ TA DUMU.MEŠ KUR-*aš-šur*
^{9}⸢LÚ⸣ [*qà*]*l-lu* LÚ *dan-*⸢*nu*$^{!}$⸣ *man-nu šá ina* ŠÀ *a-de-e*
^{10}⸢*an-nu*⸣*te šá* MÍ.*za-ku-u-te* MÍ.KUR *ina* UGU
^{11}[^{m}*aš-šur*-D]Ù-A DUMU ŠÀ-ŠÀ-*bi-šá* ḪÚL TA UN.MEŠ KUR *gab-bu*
^{12}[*taš-k*]*un-u-ni man-nu šá a-bu-tá la de-iq-tú*
^{13}[*la ṭ*]*a-ab-tú ù na-bal-kàt-tu*
^{14}[*ina* UG]U ^{m}*aš-šur*-DÙ-⸢A MAN⸣ KUR-*aš-šur* EN-*ku-nu*
^{15}[*x x t*]*a-sa-*⸢*li*⸣*-a-ni te-ep-pa-šá-a-ni*
^{16}[*nik-l*]*u*$^{!}$ *la da-an-qu da-ba-a-bu*
^{17}[*la ṭa*]-⸢*a*⸣*-bu ina* UGU ^{m}*aš-šur*-DÙ-A MAN KUR-*aš*
^{18}[EN-*ku-nu ina* Š]À-ŠÀ-*bi-ku-nu ta-nak-kil-a-nin-ni*
^{19}[*ta-dáb-bu-b*]*a-a-ni us-su-uk-tú*
^{20}[*la de-i*]*q*$^{!}$*-tú mil-ku*$^{!!}$ *la ṭa-a-bu šá si-ḫi bar-te*
^{21}[*ina* ŠÀ-*bi-ku*]*-nu*$^{!}$ *ina* UGU ^{m}*aš-šur*-DÙ-A MAN KUR-*aš* EN-*ku-nu*
^{22}[*ta-mal-l*]*ik*$^{!}$*-a-ni ta-dáb-bu-ba-a-ni*
^{23}[TA *x x x*]*x* 2-*e ina* UGU *du-a-ki*
^{24}[*šá* ^{m}*aš-šur*-DÙ-A MAN] KUR-*aš* EN-*ku-nu ta-dáb-bu-ba-a-*[*ni*]
^{25}[*aš-šur* ^{d}30 ^{d}UTU] ^{d}SAG.ME.GAR ^{d}*dil-bat*
^{e26}[^{d}UDU.IDIM.SAG].⸢UŠ⸣$^{!}$ $^{d!}$⸢UDU⸣$^{!}$.[IDI]M$^{!}$.GUD.[UD]
^{27}[^{d}*ṣal-bat*]-⸢*a*$^{!}$⸣-[*nu* ^{d}GAG.SI.SÁ *x x x*]
two lines destroyed

rev.

^{1}[*x x x x* Z]AG$^{?}$ ⸢*ù*⸣ [KAB *x x*]
^{2}[*ù šum-ma*] *at-tu-nu* TA ŠÀ$^{!!}$ UD-*me an-ni-*⸢*e*⸣
^{3}[*a-bu-tú la*] *de-iq-tú šá si-ḫi bar-te*
^{4}[*šá ina* UGU ^{m}]*aš-šur*-DÙ-A MAN KUR-*aš be-lí-ku-nu*
^{5}[*i-dáb-bu*]*-bu-u-ni* (*ta-šam-ma-a-ni*) *la tal-la-ka-nin- ni*

[45] Tadmor suggests that "... the extraordinary measures for the succession of 672, with the royal propaganda acompanying it, proved not to be sufficient. Upon Esarhaddon's death, the grandmother Naqi'a-Zakutu, imposed the *adê*-oaths once again ..." (Tadmor, *HHI*: 47).

[46] Transliteration and translation from the most recent edition of the text in Parpola and Watanabe, *SAA* II, 8.

6 [*uz-ni*] *šá* MÍ.*za-ku-u-te* AMA-*šú ù šá* ^{m}*aš-šur*-DÙ-A
7 [MAN KUR-*aš* E]N-*ku-nu la tu-pat-ta-a-ni* ⸢*ù*⸣ [*š*]*um-ma*
8 [*at-tu*]-*nu šá da-a-ki ù ḫul-lu-qi*
9 [*šá* ^{m}*aš-šur*]-DÙ-A MAN KUR-*aš* EN-*ku-nu ta-šam-ma-a-ni*
10 [*la ta*]*l-la-ka-nin-ni uz-ni šá* MÍ.*za-ku-te* 0!
11 [AMA-*šú*] ⸢*ù*⸣ *šá* ^{m}*aš-šur*-DÙ-A MAN KUR-*aš be-lí-ku-nu*
12 [*la tu-pa*]*t-ta-a-ni ù šum-ma at-tu-u*
13 [*ki-i nik-l*]*u la da-an-qu ina* UGU ^{m}*aš-šur*-DÙ-A
14 ⸢MAN KUR-*aš be-lí*⸣-*ku-nu i-nak-kil-an-ni*
15 *ta-šam-ma-a-ni la tal-la-ka-nin-ni*
16 *ina* IGI MÍ.*za-ku-te* AMA-*šú ù ina* IGI ^{m}*aš-šur*-DÙ-A
17 ⸢MAN KUR-*aš be-lí*⸣-*ku-nu la ta-qab-ba-a-ni*
18 *ù šum-ma at-tu-nu ta-šam-ma-a-ni*
19 *tu-da-a-ni ma!-a* ERIM.MEŠ *mu-šam-ḫi-iṣ-ṣu-u-te*
20 *mu-šad-bi-bu-u-te* [[*šá*]] *ina bir-tuk-ku-nu lu-u*
21 *ina* LÚ *šá ziq-ni lu-u ina* LÚ.SAG.MEŠ-*ku-nu lu-u ina* PAB.MEŠ-*šú*
22 *lu-u ina* NUMUN MAN *lu-u* PAB.MEŠ-*ku-nu lu-u* EN *ṭa-ba!-te-ku-nu*
23 [*lu-u*] *ina* UN.M[EŠ K]UR *gab-bu ta-šam-ma-a-ni*
24 [*tu-da-a-ni l*]*a ta-ṣab-ba-ta-nin-ni*
25 [*la ta-du-ka-ni ina*] ⸢UGU MÍ⸣.*za-ku-t*[*e*]!
e26 [AMA-*šú ù ina* UGU ^{m}*aš-šur*-DÙ]-⸢A⸣ [MAN KUR-*aš*]
e27 [*be-lí-ku-nu la tu-bal*]-⸢*a*!⸣-*n*[*in-ni*]

The treaty of Zakutu, the queen of Sennacherib, king of Assyria, mother of Esarhaddon, king of Assyria, with Šamaš-šumu-ukin, his equal brother, with Šamaš-metu-uballiṭ and the rest of his brothers, with the royal seed, with the magnates and the governors, the bearded and the eunuchs, the royal entourage, with the exempts and all who enter the Palace, with the Assyrians high and low:

Anyone who (is included) in this treaty which Queen Zakutu has concluded with the whole nation concerning her favorite grandson Ashurbanipal, anyone who should [...] fabricate and carry out an ugly and evil thing or a revolt against your lord Ashurbanipal, king of Assyria, in your hearts conceive and put into words an ugly scheme or an evil plot against your lord Ashurbanipal, king of Assyria, in your hearts deliberate and formulate an ugly suggestion and evil advice for rebellion and insurrection against your lord Ashurbanipal, king of Assyria, or plot with another [...] for the murder of your lord Ashurbanipal, king of Assyria:

May Aššur, Sin, Šamaš, Jupiter, Venus, Saturn Mercury, Mars and Sirius ... (break) ... south and north.

And if you from this day on (hear) an ugly word of rebellion and insurrection being spoken against your lord Ashurbanipal, king of Assyria, you shall come and inform Zakutu his mother and Ashurbanipal, king of Assyria, your lord; and if you hear of (a plan) to kill or eliminate your lord Ashurbanipal, king of Assyria, you shall come and inform Zakutu his mother and your lord Ashurbanipal, king of Assyria;

> and if you hear of an ugly scheme being elaborated against your lord Ashurbanipal, king of Assyria, you shall speak out in the presence of Zakutu his mother and your lord, Ashurbanipal, king of Assyria;
>
> and if you hear and know that there are men instigating armed rebellion or fomenting conspiracy in your midst, be they bearded or eunuchs or his brothers or of royal line or your brothers or friends or any one in the entire nation – should you hear and know, you shall seize and kill them and bring them to Zakutu his mother and to Ashurbanipal, king of Assyria, your lord.

It is clear from the treaty itself that the queen mother was taking Esarhaddon's place (temporarily) as Ashurbanipal's patron and reaffirming the succession treaty of 672. She is carrying out the stipulation in the "vassal-treaties" that calls for Ashurbanipal to be helped to take the throne when his father dies.[47] In obverse line 11 of the Zakutu treaty, the queen mother refers to Ashurbanipal as her "favorite grandson." Since Ashurbanipal is known to have been Esarhaddon's favorite, we may regard Naqia's statement as a reiteration of the late king's sentiment,[48] rather than as the prime reason for her support.[49] Likewise, the fact that Naqia always names herself first as the person to whom sedition and treason should be reported (you should speak out in the presence of Zakutu his mother and Ashurbanipal, the king, your lord (ll. 12-17 etc.), simply reflects the fact that she is imposing the treaty. It cannot be taken to mean that she had great influence over Ashurbanipal.

There is no evidence that Ashurbanipal had any difficulty whatsoever in taking his rightful place on the Assyrian throne. On the contrary, the first few years of his reign are described in the sources as a time of peace and prosperity – a golden age.[50] Although it is true that Šamaš-šumu-ukin is named in the Zakutu treaty as the primary oath-taker, which might lead one to conclude that there was already reason to question his loyalty, the sources do not support such a conclusion.[51] In fact, there does not seem to have been a pressing need for the queen mother to impose a loyalty oath. Unless we see the Zakutu treaty as part of a plan that was implemented automatically when the king died, it is difficult to imagine why anyone other than Ashurbanipal

---

47 Parpola and Watanabe, *SAA* II, 6 §7:84-85.

48 Borger, *Asarh.*: 71-72, §43: 25: [m]*aš-šur-bani-apli mār šarri rabû ša bīt ri-du-ti mār na-ram-ia* ... (Ashurbanipal, crown prince of the succession house, my beloved son ...).

49 Ben-Barak seems to interpret this to mean that "it was by her influence that her grandson, Ashurbanipal was chosen as king" (Z. Ben-Barak, "The Queen Consort and the Struggle for Succession to the Throne," *CRRAI* 33 [1986]: 37).

50 In particular see Parpola, *SAA* X, 226 = *LAS* I, 121 and Streck, *Assurbanipal*: 212.

51 Note Frame's comment that "There is no concrete evidence that relations between Ashurbanipal and Šamaš-šumu-ukin were anything but good until rebellion broke out in 652" (Frame, *Babylonia*: 108). For the relationship between the two brothers and the events leading up to the civil war of 652-648 see especially Frame, *Babylonia*: 102-30; S. Ahmed, "Causes of Shamash-shum-ukin's Uprising, 652-652 B.C.," *Zeitschrift für alttestamentliche Wissenschaft* 79 (1967): 1-13; Brinkman, *Prelude*: 85-92.

would have imposed the oath; when Esarhaddon took the throne under very difficult circumstances it was he who required his subjects to swear an oath, not his mother.[52]

In spite of the stresses she endured toward the end of Esarhaddon's reign, Naqia was able to carry out the task that had been assigned to her. Even though the situation in Assyria probably did not require the reaffirmation of Ashurbanipal as rightful king, Naqia imposed the loyalty oath. She and Esarhaddon had prepared for the worst. They expected that there would be trouble after Esarhaddon died and they set the queen mother up as an authority figure who could put Ashurbanipal on the throne. When Esarhaddon died that is exactly what Naqia did. Having discharged her duty, Naqia apparently retired from public/court life. We do not know when she died, but it seems likely that she did not long outlive her son.

---

52 Parpola and Watanabe, *SAA* II, 4.

CONCLUSION

Our study of Naqia/Zakutu has led to a reassessment of her political role. We have shown that previous scholarship was correct in viewing Naqia as a powerful force behind the throne of her son, but incorrect in attributing her position to a combination of her forceful personality and Esarhaddon's weakness. The issue is much more complex. Naqia was given her position for a reason, the roots of which are to be found in the events surrounding Esarhaddon's tenure as crown prince and the murder of his father, Sennacherib.

Naqia, whose name is West Semitic, but whose origins remain obscure, joined Sennacherib's harem by the penultimate decade of the 8th century and bore a son, Esarhaddon in c. 713. After the murder of Sennacherib's eldest son, Aššur-nadin-šumi, in 694, Sennacherib waited almost eleven years before designating another heir. When he did name his successor he promoted his youngest son, Esarhaddon, to the post, thus supplanting Urad-Mullissu who, as eldest living son, had expected to succeed his father. Urad-Mullissu had enjoyed eleven years of prominence and expectation, only to have his rank taken from him. During the brief period when Esarhaddon was crown prince (roughly two years), he and his mother had to strive constantly to maintain their positions. Eventually, Esarhaddon was forced to go into hiding. Naqia does not appear in our sources until Esarhaddon's promotion and it is not certain when, if at all, Naqia achieved first wife status. There is no indication that Naqia was influential or wielded political power at any time during Sennacherib's reign.

Ultimately, Sennacherib's decision to promote Esarhaddon led to murder and civil war. In 681 Urad-Mullissu, probably with the aid of one or more of his brothers, murdered his father and tried to take the throne. After a civil war of about six weeks duration, Esarhaddon triumphed, but his brothers were not apprehended and fled the country.

The effect that this episode had on Esarhaddon and his mother must not be underestimated. Esarhaddon's preoccupation with rebellion and the succession may be seen as a direct result of his own experiences. In order to safeguard the throne against rebellion and to ensure a smooth change of power when he died, Esarhaddon needed the support of someone with unquestionable loyalty and prestige. The only person who could fill such a position was his own mother. Her loyalty was certain, but her status at the beginning of Esarhaddon's reign was not sufficiently prominent. Naqia could not lend

Esarhaddon support unless the court and government officials accepted her as someone whose position was second only to the king's.

For this reason, Esarhaddon implemented a program that would lend his mother the prestige she needed. By associating himself with his mother, Esarhaddon was able to insinuate that Naqia was nearly as exalted as he. Thus, many of the things Naqia did were reflections of the king's actions. She built a palace for Esarhaddon and commemorated it with a building inscription in the royal style; she gave jewelry to temples for the adornment of the gods' statues; she had rituals enacted on her behalf and may have sponsored temple restoration. Her statue was placed in a temple and she was depicted with the king on a religious relief. In every case, Naqia's activities accompanied similar actions of the king. Thus, for example, when Esarhaddon built at Nineveh, she built there; he restored the temple of Sin at Harran and she worked on a temple there. Naqia even contributed to work in Babylonia.

Evidence of Naqia's status is not restricted to building and participation in various cults. She is known to have corresponded with high officials in Assyria and Babylonia, although in no case do these letters indicate that she held an official position of authority over them. It was necessary that court officials know and respect Naqia, and the letters indicate that Esarhaddon's efforts to give his mother prestige of royal proportions were successful, for his officials granted Naqia the same measure of respect and deference that they bestowed on him. Not coincidentally, virtually all of our evidence dates to the period 672-669, the same period that Esarhaddon actively promoted Ashurbanipal and Šamaš-šumu-ukin as the crown princes.

The final element in our theory that Naqia had the key role in Esarhaddon's effort to safeguard the throne and ensure the succession is the Zakutu treaty, the loyalty oath that Naqia imposed, just after Esarhaddon's death, on behalf of Ashurbanipal. This treaty marks the end of Naqia's public life, not the beginning of a new phase, as has sometimes been suggested. The Zakutu treaty is the final stroke in a plan that was put into action by the middle of Esarhaddon's reign, if not earlier. It has sometimes been suggested that Esarhaddon's fears about rebellion and the succession bordered on the paranoid, but the fact remains that his careful planning paid off. The succession was accomplished without trouble of any kind and the situation in Assyria and Babylonia remained stable for another seventeen years.

Although the evidence does not allow us to make any conclusive statements about the relationship between Esarhaddon and his mother, or about Naqia's character, it seems certain that Esarhaddon, rather than Naqia, had the dominant role. Naqia's continued commitment to Esarhaddon through the years, during periods of ill health, uncertainty and sometimes turmoil, reveals her devotion to her son.

APPENDIX A

A Catalog of Sources for Naqia/Zakutu

The following is a catalog of documentary sources for Naqia/Zakutu. The texts are grouped according to type, thus: letters, inscriptions, legal texts and so forth. Within these groups each text is designated by museum number, followed by

(I) publication of cuneiform copies or photographs,
(II) partial and full editions of the texts (transliterations and/or translations) and
(III) discussion of texts.

Category (III) may not contain every instance that a given text has been mentioned.

For letters I give length, author, addressee, a date if one has been proposed, and the script in which the letter was written (Assyrian or Babylonian). Other sources are identified by brief description (as in the case of the bronze relief) or subject (e.g. sale of slaves). Texts are dated wherever possible and arranged chronologically within each group. Abbreviations follow the rest of the volume. Full references can be found in the bibliography.

Letters

Bu 89-4-26,5

Letter; 27 lines.
Nergal-šarrani to the queen mother.
Assyrian script.
(I) Harper, *ABL* 368.
(II) Waterman, *RCAE* 368; Schmidtke, *AOTU* I/II, pp. 125-27; Winckler, *AOF* II, p. 187; Cole and Machinist, *SAA* XIII, 76.
(III) Behrens, *ABB*, pp. 8f., 35, 39 and 83[3]; Streck, *VAB,* p. cxl; Oppenheim, *JAOS* 61, pp. 261 and 270; Menzel, *Tempel*, p. 296; Matsushima, *Acta Sumerologica* 9, pp. 138f; Parpola, *LAS* 2, p. 300.

K980

Letter; 13 lines.
[Nergal-šarrani] to the queen mother.

Assyrian script.
(I) Harper, *ABL* 569.
(II) Waterman, *RCAE* 569; Schmidtke, *AOTU* I/II, p. 127; Cole and Machinst, *SAA* XIII, 77.
(III) Behrens, *ABB,* pp. 8-9; Streck, *Assurbanipal*, p. cxl; Parpola, *LAS* 2, p. 300; Boncquet, *AOB* 4, p. 189.

K486
Letter; 16 lines.
The king (Esarhaddon) to the queen mother.
Assyrian script.
(I) Harper, *ABL* 303.
(II) Waterman, *RCAE* 303; Schmidtke, *AOTU* I/II, p. 125;Winckler, *AOF* II. p. 188.
(III) Parpola, *LAS* 2. p. 131; Boncquet, *AOB* 4, p. 190.

83-1-18,271
Letter fragment; 15 lines preserved.
Issar-šumu-ereš to the queen mother.
Assyrian script.
Date: 670?
(I) Harper, *ABL* 677.
(II) Waterman, *RCAE* 677; Parpola, *LAS* 21; Parpola, *SAA* X, 16.
(III) Streck, *Assurbanipal*, p. cxl; Parpola, *LAS* 2, p. 27; Boncquet, *AOB* 4, p. 188.

K5486
Letter fragment; 8 lines preserved.
Issar-šumu-ereš to the queen mother.
Assyrian script.
Date: 670?
(I) Parpola, *CT* 53, 84.
(II) Parpola, *LAS* 230; Parpola, *SAA* X, 17.
(III) Parpola, *LAS* 2. pp. 220-21.

82-5-22,152 + 83-1-18,66
Letter; 57 lines.
Unknown author to the queen mother.
Assyrian script.
(I) Parpola, *CT* 53, 921.
(II) ; Cole and Machinst, *SAA* XIII, 188
(III) Parpola, *LAS* 2, p. 299.

K1527
Letter; 11 lines partially preserved. Very badly broken.
Unknown author to the queen mother?

Assyrian script.
(I) Parpola, *CT* 53, 182.

K1355

Letter; 33 lines preserved.
Na'id-Marduk to the queen mother.
Babylonian script.
Date: c. 675?
(I) Harper, *ABL* 917.
(II) Waterman, *RCAE* 917; Dietrich, *AOAT* 7, pp. 144-45 and 148-49.
(III) Streck, *VAB*, p. cxl; Lewy, *JNES* 11, p. 274; Dietrich, *AOAT* 7, pp. 26-27, 33 and 38-39; Boncquet, *AOB* 4, p. 189; Porter, Images, p. 35, n. 76.

K478

Letter; 18 lines.
Ašaredu to the queen mother.
Babylonian script.
(I) Harper, *ABL* 254.
(II) Waterman, *RCAE* 254; Delitzsch, *BA* I, p. 189; Smith, *PSBA* (1887): V, p. 9; Schmidtke, *AOTU* I/II, p. 129; Winckler, *AOF* II, p. 189.
(III) Streck, *VAB*, p. cxl; Dietrich, *WO* 4, p. 219; Dietrich, *AOAT* 7, p. 53f; Boncquet, *AOB* 4, p. 188; *PNA* 1/I, p. 141.

K825

Letter; 19 lines.
Nabû-šumu-lišir to the queen mother.
Babylonian script
Date: Du'uzu, 671?
(I) Harper, *ABL* 263.
(II) Waterman, *RCAE* 263; Schmidtke, *AOTU* I/II, p. 129; Winckler, *AOF* II, p. 188; Parpola, *SAA* X, 313.
(III) Behrens, *ABB*, p. 13; Streck, *VAB*, p. cxl; Menzel, *Tempel* p. 295 and n. 3943; Boncquet, *AOB* 4, p. 189.

K523

Letter; 19 lines.
Aplâ to the queen mother.
Babylonian script.
(I) Harper, *ABL* 324.
(II) Waterman, *RCAE* 324; Delitzsch, *BA* I, p. 192; Smith, *PSBA*, pl. II, p. 5; Schmidtke, *AOTU* I/II, p. 127-28; Winckler, *AOF* II, p. 188; Parpola, *SAA* X, 154.
(III) Streck, *VAB*, p. cxxxix; Lewy, *JNES* 11, p. 274, n. 49; Boncquet, *AOB* 4, p. 188-89; *PNA* 1/I, p. 116, no. 19.

82-5-22,105

Letter; c. 47 lines.
Bel-ušezib to the king (Esarhaddon).
The queen mother is mentioned in obv. 14.
Babylonian script.
Date: 680 (Labat, *RA* 53, p. 114; Parpola, *CRRAI* 26, p. 179).
(I) Harper, *ABL* 1216.
(II) Waterman, *RCAE* 1216; Schmidtke, *AOTU* I/II, p. 106-107. Labat, *RA* 53, p. 114ff; Oppenheim, *JAOS* 61, p. 265; Parpola, *LAS* 2, p. 50; Parpola, *SAA* X, 109; Nissinen, *SAAS* 7, p. 89.
(III) Parpola, *CRRAI* 26, p. 179; Cogan, *HHI*, p. 82; Dietrich, *AOAT* 7, p. 50, 63-64, 67-68 and 152; Postgate, *Taxation*, p. 152; Boncquet, *AOB* 4, p. 191; Nissinen, *SAAS* 7, pp. 89-95.

K538

Letter; 32 lines.
Urad-Nabû to the king.
The queen mother is mentioned in rev. 4.
Assyrian script.
Date: 672-669.
(I) Harper, *ABL* 114
(II) Waterman, *RCAE* 114; Cole and Machinist, *SAA* XIII, 61.
(III) Deller, *OrNS* 31, p. 11; Boncquet, *AOB* 4, p. 191.

Ki 1904-10-9,48

Letter; 23 lines.
Marduk-šakin-šumi to the king (Esarhaddon).
The queen mother is mentioned obv. 11 and rev. 7.
Assyrian script.
Date: June, 670 (Parpola, *LAS* 2, p. 174).
(I) Harper, *ABL* 1388.
(II) Waterman, *RCAE* 1388; Parpola, *LAS* 184; Parpola, *SAA* X, 244.
(III) Parpola, *LAS* 2, pp. 174-76; Boncquet, *AOB* 4, p. 191.

83-1-18,106

Letter; c. 19 lines.
Nabû-naṣir and Urad-Nanâ to the king (Esarhaddon).
The queen mother is mentioned obv. 9.
Date: June, 670 (Parpola, *LAS* 2, p. 215).
Assyrian script.
(I) Harper, *ABL* 719.
(II) Waterman, *RCAE* 719; Parpola, *LAS* 222; Parpola, *SAA* X, 297.
(III) Parpola, *LAS* 2, p. 215; Boncquet, *AOB* 4, p. 190.

Bu 91-5-9,15

Letter; 20 lines preserved.
Adad-šumu-uṣur to the king (Esarhaddon).

The queen mother is mentioned obv. 6.
Assyrian script.
Date: June?, 670 (Parpola, *LAS* 2, p. 146).
(I) Harper, *ABL* 660.
(II) Waterman, *RCAE* 660; Parpola, *LAS* 159; Parpola, *SAA* X, 200.
(III) Behrens, *ABB*, p. 93;[2] Oppenheim *JAOS* 64, 194; Parpola, *LAS* 2, pp. 146-47; Boncquet, *AOB* 4, p. 190; *PNA* 1/I, p. 38.

K611

Letter; 20 lines preserved.
Adad-šumu-uṣur to the king (Esarhaddon).
The queen mother is mentioned obv. 7.
Assyrian script.
Date: June?, 670 (Parpola, *LAS* 2, p. 148).
(I) Harper, *ABL* 549.
(II) Waterman, *RCAE* 549; Parpola, *LAS* 160; Parpola, *SAA* X, 201.
(III) Behrens, *ABB,* p. 18; Dhorme, *RHR* 113, p. 148; Deller, *AOAT* I, p. 55; Parpola, *LAS* 2, p. 148; Boncquet, *AOB* 4, p. 190; *PNA* 1/I, p. 38.

K649

Letter; 21 lines.
Nabû-nadin-šumi to the king (Esarhaddon).
The queen mother is mentioned rev. 7.
Assyrian script.
Date: late Abu 670 (Parpola, *LAS* 2, p. 203)
(I) Harper *ABL* 56.
(II) Waterman, *RCAE* 56; Parpola, *LAS* 208; Parpola, *SAA* X, 274.
(III) Behrens, *ABB*, p. 103; Dhorme, *RHR* 116, p. 20; Labat, *Royauté*, p. 151; Abusch, *JNES* 33, p. 259-61; Parpola, *LAS* 2,pp. 203-204; Boncquet, *AOB* 4, p. 191.

Bu 91-5-9,183

Letter; 46 lines.
Mar-Issar to the king (Esarhaddon).
The queen mother is mentioned obv. 13.
Date: 671-V-2 (Parpola, *LAS* 2, p. 264).
(I) Harper, *ABL* 340.
(II) Waterman, *RCAE* 340; Parpola, *LAS* 276; Parpola, *SAA* X, 348.
(III) Weidner, *AfO* 13, p. 55; Landsberger, *BBEA,* pp. 53-54; Parpola *LAS* 2, p. 264; Boncquet, *AOB* 4, p. 191.

K1101 + K1221

Letter; 32 lines.
Dadî to the crown prince (Ashurbanipal).
The queen mother is mentioned in rev. 8.
Assyrian script.

Date: 672-669.
(I) Harper, *ABL* 152
(II) Waterman, *RCAE* 152; Oppenheim, *LFM*, p. 182; Cole and Machinist, *SAA* XIII, 154.
(III) Oppenheim, *BASOR* 107, p. 9; Deller, *OrNS* 34, 383; Streck, *VAB* 817; Menzel, *Tempel*, p. 103; Postgate, *Taxation*, p. 151.

K549

Letter (horse report); 13 lines.
Nabû-šumu-iddina to the king (Esarhaddon).
The queen mother is mentioned in obv. 8.
Assyrian script.
(I) Harper, *ABL* 63.
(II) Waterman, *RCAE* 63; Cole and Machinist, *SAA* XIII, 101.
(III) Postgate, *Taxation*, p. 8; Boncquet, *AOB* 4, p. 190.

Ki 1904-10-9,33

Letter (horse report); 24 lines.
Nabû-šumu-iddina to the king (Esarhaddon).
The queen mother is mentioned in obv. 8.
Assyrian script.
(I) Harper, *ABL* 1379.
(II) Waterman, *RCAE* 1379; Cole and Machinist, *SAA* XIII, 90.
(III) Postgate, *Taxation,* p. 8; Boncquet, *AOB* 4, p. 190.

80-7-19,25

Letter (horse report); 25 lines.
Nadinu to the king (Esarhaddon).
The queen mother is mentioned in rev. 3.
Assyrian script.
(I) Harper, *ABL* 393.
(II) Waterman, *RCAE* 393; Cole and Machinist, *SAA* XIII, 108.
(III) Postgate, *Taxation,* p. 9; Boncquet, *AOB* 4, p. 190.

K14680

Letter fragment; 7 lines partially preserved (only a couple of signs per line).
The word *šarratim* appears in line 2 and Dietrich takes this as a reference to the queen, "perhaps Naqia/Zakutu."
(I) Dietrich, *CT* 54, 279.
(III) Dietrich, *WO* 4, p. 203.

K2909

Letter; 19 lines preserved.
Issar-šumu-ereš to the king (Esarhaddon).
The queen mother is possibly mentioned in obv. 10 and rev. 7.

Assyrian script.
(I) Harper, *ABL* 41.
(II) Waterman, *RCAE* 41; Parpola, *LAS* 20; Parpola, *SAA* X, 28.

Naqia's building inscriptions

K2745 + Rm 494

Fragments of a five-sided prism, K2745 = Bezold, *Cat.*, p. 471; Rm 494 = Bezold, *Cat.*, p. 1617.
(II) Meissner and Rost, *BA* III, pp. 208-209 and 285; Luckenbill, *ARAB*, §614 and §700A; Borger, *Asarh.*, §86.
(III) Boncquet, *AOB* 4, p. 186.

81-2-4,173

Fragment of a 'prismoid,' 81-2-4,173 = Bezold, *Cat.*, p. 1768.
(II) Meissner and Rost, *BA* III, pp. 208-209 and 285; Luckenbill, *ARAB*, §614 and §700A; Borger, *Asarh.*, §86.
(III) Boncquet, *AOB* 4, p. 186.

91-5-9,217

Fragment of a 'barrel cylinder,' 91-5-9,217
(II) Borger, *ARRIM* 6, pp. 7 and 11.

Monumental inscription/relief

AO 20.185

Bronze plaque with bas relief depicting king followed by woman identified as Naqia (name inscribed on her shoulder).
(II-III) Parrot and Nougayrol, *Syria* 33, pp. 147-60 and pl .6; Parrot and Nougayrol, *Revue des Arts* 3, pp. 98ff; Gadd, *AnSt* 8, p. 41; Parrot, *Assur*, p. 118; Hallo, *BA* 23, p. 54; Hrouda, *HdArch* p. 243, pl. 105; Weidner, *AfO* 21, p. 130; Börker-Klähn, *ABVF* nos. 220-21; Braun-Holzinger, *FBM* p. 105 and pl. 68-69; Curtis, *Bronzeworking*, pp. 88-89 and fig. 87; Boncquet, *AOB* 4, p. 186; Frahm, Sanherib, pp. 169-70.

Dedicatory inscriptions

82-5-22,90

Tablet inscribed with copies of two dedicatory inscriptions of Naqia.
(I) Johns, *ADD* 645.
(II) Meissner, *MDVAG* 8/3, pp. 98-99; Kohler and Ungnad, *ARU* 14;

(III) Meissner, *MDVAG* 8/3, p. 96-97; Schmidtke, *AOTU* I/II, p. 124; Streck, *VAB* p. ccxxvii; Lewy, *JNES* 11, p. 273; Borger, *BiOr* 29, p. 34; Borger, *ARRIM* 6, p. 7; Boncquet, *AOB* 4, p. 185.

Banded agate bead

Bead inscribed with the name Naqia. Part of a private collection.
(II) Scheil, *RT* 20, p. 200 no. 8.; Galter, *ARRIM* 5, no. 44.
(III) Lewy, *JNES* 11, p. 272, n. 41; Van De Mieroop, *Hallo Fest.*, p. 259; Boncquet, *AOB* 4, p. 185; Frahm, Sanherib, p. 149.

Banded agate bead

Bead with dedicatory inscription of Naqia.
Part of the Jonathan Rosen collection.
(I) Van De Mieroop, *Hallo Fest.*, p. 260 (copy) and 261 (photo).
(II) Van De Mieroop, *Hallo Fest.*, pp. 259-60; Frahm, Sanherib, p. 149.

Economic and administrative documents[1]

K2696 + 81-7-27,113 + 80-7-19,111

Grant of queen mother's estate at Šabbu to the queen.
Date: 683-681.
(I) Johns, *ADD* 666 + 739 + 738.
(II) Kohler and Ungnad, *ARU* 12 + 27 + 25; Postgate, *NARGD* 34-36; Kataja and Whiting, *SAA* XII, 21-23.
(III) Postgate, *NARGD* pp. 70-73; Kataja and Whiting, *SAA* XII, pp. xxiv-xxv. See also Sachs, *Iraq* 16, p. 172; van Driel, *BiOr* 27, p. 174; Boncquet, *AOB* 4, p. 193; Frahm, Sanherib, pp. 241-42.

82-5-22,34

Queen's village manager sells people and an orchard.
Date: 683-II-1.
(I) Johns, *ADD* 447.
(II) Kohler and Ungnad, *ARU* 61; Kwasman, *NALK* 14; Kwasman and Parpola, *SAA* VI, 90.

K1617

The village manager of the queen mother sells people.
Date: 678.
(I) Johns, *ADD* 301.
(II) Kohler and Ungnad, *ARU* 535; Parpola, *Assur* 5/2, p. *** (collations); Kwasman and Parpola, *SAA* VI, 255.
(III) Streck, *VAB* ccxxviii and cxl; Lewy, *JNES* 11, pp. 273-74; Borger, *BiOr* 29, pp. 33-34; Boncquet, *AOB* 4, pp. 186 and 192.

[1] See Appendix B for a detailed discussion of these texts and their contents.

Assur 13956[bq]

Ration list – disbursement of goods.
Queen mother mentioned obv. 4.
Date: 672-669.
(I) Weidner, *AfO* 13, pl.xiv.
(II-III) Weidner, *AfO* 13, p. 214; Menzel, *Tempel* II, no. 15, T17-T18.

K324

The queen mother's scribe sells part of a village.
Date: 663-X-25.
(I) Johns, *ADD* 470.
(II) Kohler and Ungnad, *ARU* 168; Kwasman, *NALK* 256; Kwasman and Parpola, *SAA* VI, 325.

K1359+K13197

List of officials.
(I) Johns, *ADD* 857; Bezold, *PSBA* 11, pls. IV-V; Fales and Postgate, *SAA* VII, pl. I (photo).
(II) Kinnier Wilson, *NWL*, pp. 101-104; Fales and Postgate, *SAA* VII, 5.
(III) Kinnier Wilson, *NWL*, pp. 100-104; Postgate, *Taxation*, p. 194; Fales and Postgate, *SAA* VII, xvii-xix; Boncquet, *AOB* 4, p. 193.

K7387 + K12843 + 82-3-23,99

List of officials.
(I) Johns, *ADD* 840 + 858; Fales and Postgate, *SAA* VII, pl. I (photo).
(II) Fales and Postgate, *SAA* VII, 6; Boncquet, *AOB* 4, p. 193.

K8143 + 80-7-19,105

List of lodgings for officials.
(I) Johns, *ADD* 860; Fales and Postgate, *SAA* VII, pl. II (photo).
(II) Fales and Postgate, *SAA* VII, 9.
(III) Postgate, *Taxation*, p. 140; Boncquet, *AOB* 4, p. 193.

81-2-4,490

List of lodgings for officials.
(I) Johns, *ADD* 866.
(II) Fales and Postgate, *SAA* VII, 12; Boncquet, *AOB* 4, p. 193.

K1493

Silver payments to do with the queen mother.[2]
(I) Johns, *ADD* 1075.
(II) Fales and Postgate, *SAA* VII, 48.

[2] The text is not dated and the prosopography does not allow us to be sure about the general period to which it belongs.

Queries to Šamaš

K11491

Query about the appointment of a bodyguard for Naqia.
Babylonian script.
(II) Knudtzon, *AGS* 130; Starr, *SAA* IV, 151.

83-1-18,536 + Ki 1904-10-9,16 (BM98987)

Query as to whether Naqia's illness will pass.
Assyrian script.
(II) Knudtzon, *AGS* 101 (+); Starr, *SAA* IV, 190.
(III) Aro, *CRRAI* 14, p. 116; Parpola, *LAS* 2, pp. 215 and 237.

K11487

Query that might refer to the queen mother's illness.[3]
Babylonian script.
(II) Knudtzon, *AGS* 102; Starr, *SAA* IV, 191.

Adê agreement

83-1-18,45 + 83-1-18,266

Loyalty oath of queen dowager Zakutu on behalf of her grandson Ashurbanipal.
Date: Arahsamna/Kislev 669 (Parpola, *JCS* 39, p. 168).
(I) Harper, *ABL* 1239 + Parpola, *JCS* 189 (photo).
(II) Waterman, *AJSL* 29, 1ff.; Lewy, *JNES* 11, n. 92; Parpola, *JCS* 39, pp. 165-67; Parpola and Watanabe, *SAA* II, 8.
(III) Streck, *Assurbanipal*, p. ccxxvii; Lewy, *JNES* 11, pp. 282-284; Parpola, *JCS* 39, pp. 167-68; Parpola and Watanabe, *SAA* II, pp. xxxi-xxxii, and xlviii-xlix.

Oracles

K4310 (v 12-23)

Oracle of Aḫat-abiša of Arbela concerning Esarhaddon.
Addressed to the king and the queen mother.
(I) Pinches, 4R^2 61; Parpola, *SAA* IX, pls. I-III (photos).
(II) Banks, *AJSL* 14, p. 275-76; Delattre, *The Babylonian and Oriental Record* III, pp. 25-31; Schmidtke, *AOTU* I/II, p. 122; Biggs, *ANET* II, p. 169; Parpola, *SAA* IX, 1.8; Nissinen, *SAAS* 7, pp. 22-23.

---

[3] See Starr, *SAA* IV, p. 194, n. 2.

(III) Weippert, *ARINH*, pp. 112-15; Parpola, *Murderer*, n. 40; Parpola, *SAA* IX, pp. xliii, il and lxviii; Nissinen, *SAAS* 7, pp. 22-23.

K6259

Oracle of Issar of Arbela addressed to a woman, probably the queen mother (Weippert, *ARINH*, p. 112).
(I) Langdon, *TI*, pl.IV; Parpola, *SAA* IX, pl. VIII (photo).
(II) Parpola, *SAA* IX, 5; Nissinen, *SAAS* 7, p. 23.
(III) Weippert, *ARINH*, pp. 112-15; Parpola, *SAA* IX, p. lxx; Nissinen, *SAAS* 7, pp. 23f.

K12033 + 82-5-22,527

Seven or more oracles addressed to the king and queen mother from Issar of Arbela.
(I) Langdon, *TI*, pl. II-III; Parpola, *SAA* IX, pls. IV-V (photos).
(II) Parpola, *SAA* IX, 2.1.
(III) Weippert, *ARINH,* pp. 112-15; Parpola, *SAA* IX, p. lxix.

Seal impressions[4]

BM84789

King and queen worshipping a goddess.
(I) Reade, *CRRAI* 33, p. 144 (photo).
(III) Reade, *CRRAI* 33, pp. 144-45.

BM84802

King and queen worshipping goddess.
(I) Reade, *CRRAI* 33, p. 145 (photo).
(II) Reade, *CRRAI* 33, p. 145.

BM84671

Two women worshipping a goddess.
(I) Reade, *CRRAI* 33, p. 145 (photo).
(II) Reade, *CRRAI* 33, p. 145.

---

[4] It should be noted that nowhere on these seal impressions is Naqia identified. They may not represent her at all, but they are included here because they are discussed in Chapter II above.

APPENDIX B

Evidence for the Queen Mother's Household and Economic Obligations

The queen mother's household

Information about the size, composition and function of the queen mother's household is meager. What little we do know is gleaned from a wide variety of sources. Because there is almost no information concerning queen mothers other than Naqia,[1] it is almost impossible to generalize about the economic position of the queen mother and the obligations she held at court. For this reason, this appendix is limited to a discussion of Naqia's household and her tax obligations. We do not include evidence of the queen's household in our investigation because the queen's household included the harem and was part of the larger palace structure.[2]

There is no way of properly estimating either the capital holdings of Naqia or her income, but we do know that she had a staff of considerable size (see below); received gifts of value from the king (wood, for example[3]); and in turn gave gifts to courtiers (such as silver utensils[4]). She made costly dedications to temples[5] and was wealthy enough to build a palace for Esarhaddon. Evidence shows that she must have been extremely wealthy.

We can positively identify only two estates of the queen mother, each of which is only documented once.[6] Naqia's estate at Šabbu was discussed in

[1] In addition to the documentary evidence for Naqia (for which see Appendix A), two texts refer to the queen mother of Sennacherib (*NARGD* 34-36 [= *SAA* XII, 21-23] and *SAA* VI, 143) and one text may refer to the queen mother of Ashurbanipal (*SAA* VI, 325).

[2] Kinnier Wilson, *NWL*: 44 and 96.

[3] Borger, *Asarh.*, 116, §86, III: 5-8 and see above, Chapter III, p. 40.

[4] *SAA* XIII, 154, rev. 3-8 and above, Chapter IV, p. 76.

[5] Kohler and Ungnad, *ARU* 14 and see above Chapter III, pp. 43-44. Parpola, *SAA* X, 348, obv. 13.

[6] It is also possible that the queen mother held land in the town of Gadisê, in the vicinity of Harran. *SAA* XIII, 188 r.17-18, although badly broken, seems to indicate that a statue of the queen mother was displayed publicly there, which suggests that she may have owned an estate in the area (cf. above, p. 53, n. 93).

Chapter I: she received it when she was MÍ.É.GAL and presumably she kept it. From *SAA* VI, 255 we know that Naqia had an estate at Lahiru in northern Babylonia in 678 and that she employed a LÚ.GAL.URU.MEŠ (village manager) there, which suggests that the estate was large. There is no evidence that she ever visited either location and she may have been an absentee landlord.

In addition to the above, she undoubtedly had residences in the major Assyrian cities; Calah and Nineveh and perhaps Assur, Kilizi, Ekallate or Tarbiṣu. Although we have no documentary evidence for these residences we may infer from the sources that the queen mother did not usually live at the palace but supported a household of some size elsewhere, and further, that Naqia was able to stay close to the king when he traveled to different cities. *SAA* X, 274, a letter to Esarhaddon from Nabû-nadin-šumi asks: *a-na* MÍ.AMA LUGAL *le-e-pu-u-šu mi-i-nu ša* LUGAL *i-qab-bu-u-ni* (should I do (these rites[7]) for the queen mother? What is it that the king says?). This letter implies that the queen mother was not considered part of the royal family, for whom the rites were to be performed. She must have been visiting the palace at the time the letter was written,[8] and normally would have stayed at her own house. Assur 13956[bq], a fragmentary text which deals with the disbursement of grain or meal to members of the king's household, probably alludes to a special occasion when the royal family was in Assur for some religious festival. It might suggest that on such occasions (or perhaps when in Assur) the queen mother stayed at the palace.[9] It seems likely that Naqia herself occupied the palace at Nineveh that she built for Esarhaddon. When at Nineveh the king probably stayed in the newly renovated *ekal māšarti* or Sennacherib's palace. The numerous letters written to the queen mother from officials in Assyria and Babylonia, suggest that the she stayed close to the king.[10]

Economic and administrative documents supply us with the only information we have about the officials and functionaries attached to the queen mother's household. The following list of attested offices has been compiled from various administrative and economic documents, the pertinent lines of which are quoted later in this appendix.

ša rēši (eunuch)
masennu[11] (treasurer)
ṭupšarru (scribe)

---

[7] See rev. 2ff about the performing of periodic apotropaic rites in the month of Abu. Note too Parpola's explanation about why *lēpušu* is a first person singular and not a third person plural (*LAS* 2: 204).

[8] Parpola dates the text to late Abu = early August 670 (Parpola, *LAS* 2: 203).

[9] E.F. Weidner, "Assurbanipal in Aššur," *AfO* 13 (1939-40): 214.

[10] All the letters were found in Nineveh which strongly suggests that she usually lived there. See Borger's comments in *BiOr* 29 (1972): 34.

[11] The spelling *masennu* rather than *mašennu* follows the convention of the *SAA* series. See in particular Kwasman and Parpola, *SAA* VI, 275 where the word is written in Akkadian *ma-se-nu*.

ša pān ekalli (palace superintendent)
rab ālāni (village manager)
rab kiṣri (cohort commander)
qurbūtu (bodyguard)
ša šēpi guard
mukīl appāte (chariot driver)
tašlīšu (third man on a chariot)
šaniu ša šāqî (deputy cupbearer)
šaniu ša rab kāri (deputy chief of the quays)
rab ašlaki (chief fuller)
rab karkadinni (chief confectioner)

Some of the above offices imply the existence of associated positions. Thus the *šaniu ša šāqî* would have served the *šāqe* of the queen mother just as the *šaniu ša rab kāri* would have served the *rab kāri*. Of course the converse is true and positions on the list that begin with *rab* (chief) require that there be men subordinate to them. The existence of a *karkadinnu* in the queen mother's household also calls for the similar offices of *nuḫatimmu* (cook), *rab karāni* (wine master) and other domestic staff, including a *rab bīti* (majordomo) and *rab danibāti*[12] (chief victualler/grain purveyor).

In *SAA* VII, 5, a list of household personnel primarily of the chief eunuch, the crown prince and the queen mother, and in *SAA* VII, 6,[13] a similar list of personnel, no fewer than four different *ša rēši* (eunuchs), five *qurubūtu* (bodyguards), two *rab kiṣri* (cohort commanders), and two *mukīl appāte* (chariot drivers) belonging to her staff are named, thus giving us some idea of the scale of her household and the size of her bodyguard detachment (at least two cohorts[14]). Although these texts by no means represent the complete households of the queen mother, the crown prince and the chief eunuch, it is interesting to note the differences among them. Thus, the queen mother has four eunuchs listed while the crown prince and chief eunuch do not list any. As one would expect the crown prince and chief eunuch command many more cohorts than the queen mother: eight and six respectively. However, the queen mother lists two treasurers and a palace superintendent while the others do not, although these differences may be due to the vagaries of the list. The queen mother probably had a core staff which she kept with her when travelling from one residence to another and a permanent "skeleton" staff at each residence to see to its continued maintenance.

---

[12] For this reading see Fales and Postgate, *SAA* VII, 5, col. II, l. 50; cf. B. Menzel-Wortmann, "Der [LÚ]GAL *danibata* in neuassyrischer Zeit," *Mesopotamia* 21 (1986): 213-27.

[13] For the newest and most accurate editions of these texts see now Fales and Postgate, *SAA* VII, 5 and 9.

[14] Kinnier Wilson, *NWL*: 51. Note for comparison that the crown prince in *SAA* VII, 5 has no fewer than seven *rab kiṣri* in his household, while the chief eunuch has five.

It is impossible to give even a hypothetical estimate of the number of people who would have been supported (or partially supported) by the queen mother, although the number was probably quite substantial. According to Kinnier Wilson the queen's daily ration was for about two hundred and fifty people, but this would have included the harem.[15] In fact, it seems that the queen mother's household had the same basic structure as the queen's (minus the harem) and other royals/high officials, but even a more detailed evaluation of the available data will only produce theoretical numbers at this point.

The following is a list of the names and offices of people attached to Naqia's household, both from the time she was queen and the time she was queen mother and dowager queen mother.[16] Dated texts appear first in chronological order, followed by undated texts. When single texts have multiple references to Naqia, they are arranged according to the sequence of line numbers.

1. ^{m}*mar-tú-u*ʾ$^{!}$ LÚ.GAL URU.MEŠ *ša* MÍ(.KUR)
   Martu, village manager of the queen.
   SAA VI, 90, obv. 1. Date: 683-II-1.

2. ^{m}⸢*i*$^{!}$⸣-*du*$^{!}$-*u-a* LÚ.GAL U[RU(.MEŠ)] [*ša* UR]U *la.ḫi.ra ša* É AMA.MAN
   Idua, village manager of Lahiru of the queen mother's estate.
   SAA VI, 255, obv. 1-2. Date: 678.

3. ^{m}*as-qu*$^{!}$-*di* LÚ.A.BA ⸢*ša* AMA$^{!}$⸣.[MAN]
   Asqudi, scribe of the queen mother.
   SAA VI, 325, obv. 2. Date: 663-X-25.

4. ^{m}*aš-šur-x*[*x x x*] LÚ.SAG AMA.MAN
   Aššur-[...], eunuch of the queen mother.
   SAA VII, 5, col. I., l. 32.

5. ^{m}PAB-[*x x*] *x* LÚ.IGI.DUB$^{!}$ AMA.MAN
   Ahu-[...], treasurer of the queen mother.
   SAA VII, 5, col. I, l. 35.

6. ^{m}PA-*x*[*x x*]*x* LÚ.*šá* IGI.KUR :
   Nabû-[...], palace superintendent ditto.
   SAA VII, 5, col. I, l. 36.

7. ^{m}[*x x x x*] LÚ.*qur*-ZAG AMA.MAN
   [PN], bodyguard of the queen mother.
   SAA VII, 5, col. I, l. 42.

8. ^{m}15-I [L]Ú : :
   Issar-na'id, ditto ditto.
   SAA VII, 5, col. I, l. 43.

---

[15] Kinnier Wilson, *NWL*: 44.

[16] For full text references see Appendix A.

9. mdPA-BÀD-PAB LÚ.SAG A[MA!.MAN]
Nabû-duru-uṣur, eunuch of the queen mother.
SAA VII, 5, col. I, l. 46.

10. mIGI!-[*x x x x x*] L[Ú!.S]AG! AMA.⌜MAN!⌝
Pan-[...], eunuch of the queen mother.
SAA VII, 5, col. II, ln.16.

11. m*sa-lam-a-nu* L[Ú.GAL] *ki-ṣir* AMA.MAN
Salamanu, cohort commander of the queen mother.
SAA VII, 5, col. II, ln.30.

12. m*mu-tak-kil-aš-šur* L[Ú.*qur*-ZA]G! AMA.MAN
Mutakkil-Aššur, bodyguard of the queen mother.
SAA VII, 5, col. II, l. 32.

13. [mE]N!-PAB!-MEŠ-*šú* [LÚ].⌜3⌝-*šú* AMA.MAN!
Bel-aḫḫešu, third man of the queen mother.
SAA VII, 5, rev. col. I, l. 7.

14. mdPA-MAN-P[AB LÚ.*x* A]MA.MAN
Nabû-šarru-uṣur, [...] of the queen mother.
SAA VII, 5, rev. col. I, l. 18.

15. mdMAŠ-DINGI[R-*a-a* LÚ.*qur*.ZAG AMA.MAN
Inurta-ila'i, bodyguard of the queen mother.
SAA VII, 5, rev. col. I, l. 42.

16. [m*x x x*] LÚ.SAG AMA.MAN
[PN], eunuch of the queen mother.
SAA VII, 5, rev. col. I, l. 46.

17. m*bir-ia-ma-a* LÚ.DIB.PA.MEŠ AMA.MAN
Bir-yama, chariot driver of the queen mother.
SAA VII, 5, rev. col. II, l. 5.

18. m*il-ta-da-a-a* LÚ.DIB.PA.MEŠ AMA.MAN
Iltadaya, chariot driver of the queen mother.
SAA VII, 5, rev. col. II, l. 10.

11. mdPA-*še-zib* LÚ.GAL.SUM.NINDA AMA.MAN
Nabû-ušezib, chief confectioner of the queen mother.
SAA VII, 6, col. I, l. 8.

12. [m*x*]-*bi-i* LÚ.IGI.DUB AMA.MAN
Gabbi?, treasurer of the queen mother.
SAA VII, 9, col. I, l. 6.

13. [m*x x x x x*] LÚ.GAL *ki-ṣir* AMA.MAN
[PN], cohort commander of the queen mother.
SAA VII, 9, col. I, l. 7.

14. mdPA.TÚG-MAN-PAB LÚ.2-*ú ša* LÚ.KAŠ.LUL AMA.MAN
Nusku-šarru-uṣur, deputy cupbearer of the queen mother.
SAA VII, 9, col. I, ln.24.

15. ^{md}PA-*re-eh-tú*-PAB LÚ.[*x* AM]A$^{!}$.MAN
Nabû-rehtu-uṣur, [...] of the queen mother.
SAA VII, 9, col. II, l. 11.

16. ^{m}*ú-a-za-ru* LÚ.*qur*-ZAG AMA.MAN
Wazaru, bodyguard of the queen mother.
SAA VII, 9, rev. col. I, l. 22.

17. ^{m}DI-*mu*-EN LÚ.2-*ú* LÚ.GAL.KAR AMA.MAN
Šulmu-beli, deputy of the chief of quays of the queen mother.
SAA VII, 9, rev. col. I, ln.27.

18. [^{md}PA.T]ÚG-MAN-PAB LÚ.GAL.TÚG$^{!}$.[UD] *ša* AMA.MAN
Nusku-šarru-uṣur, chief fuller of the queen mother
SAA VII, 12, obv.3-4.

19. [*x x x*]-*a-lik-pa-ni* L[Ú.*x x*] [*ša*] AMA.MAN
[...]-alik-pani, [...] of the queen mother.
SAA VII, 12, obv.6-7.

Obligations of the queen mother

As queen mother Naqia made donations to temples and contributed horses to the palace. Some of her expenditures can be regarded as tax obligations. It is likely that such fiscal responsibilities took other forms as well, although at present there is no way to identify them.

The horse-reports from the palace archives at Nineveh provide us with some interesting comparative information about Naqia's obligation to provide horses to the palace. In three of these letters (*SAA* XIII, 90, 101 and 108) Nabû-šumu-iddina/Nadinu[17] reports to the king that the *masennu* (treasurer) of the queen mother has delivered a total of twenty Kusian horses to the palace at Nineveh.[18] When this information is considered in light of the horse-reports as a whole some important observations can be made.

For example, the only members of the royal family to be mentioned in the horse reports are the queen mother and the queen (mentioned in *SAA* XIII, 108), a fact which may be significant for purposes of dating the texts as well as determining their economic importance. Since the crown prince (or princes) does not appear in these reports, it is tempting to date them to the period

[17] On the probability that these are one and the same person see Postgate, *Taxation*: 11. and note also Parpola review of Postgate, *Taxation*. in *ZA* 65 (1975): 294, "The identity of N. and Nadinu is beyond doubt ..."

[18] In view of the fact that the queen's *masennu* also made deliveries, and no other officials of either household are mentioned, it is certain that these officials were not acting on their own behalf (i.e., paying taxes from their own estates) but were carrying out their official duties.

before the queen's death in 672. It is, however, also possible that they date to the early part of Ashurbanipal's reign, although this would require either that Ešarra-ḫammat was not his mother or that the queen mother of the reports is actually Naqia, the dowager queen mother.[19] Both Postgate and Fales remark on the ephemeral nature of these reports.[20] Postgate suggests that they all date to a single year and further points out that they date to the three months prior to the start of campaign season.[21] At present the dating of these reports remains uncertain.

The other contributors of horses seem to fall into two groups: those that can be connected to the provincial system and those that apparently have nothing to do with the provincial system. The former include: provincial governors, the *turtānu* (commander-in-chief), *nāgir ekalli* (palace herald) and *rab šāqê* (chief cupbearer); governors of the cities Assur, Calah and Nineveh; and provinces or provincial capitals by place name. The latter are comprised of the LÚ*raksu* (recruits), and the LÚ*šaknūti* (prefects). It is difficult to say just how the queen and queen mother fit into these groups. Certainly they are not contributing horses as provincial governors. However, as the highest ranking members of the royal family after the king (there was as yet no crown prince) they did own large estates of their own and their contributions must been seen as something of an estate tax.

In order to compare the number of horses the queen mother provided with those given by the other contributors (excluding those mentioned by place alone) it is necessary to reproduce Postgate's list [22] more or less in full:

turtānu	521
turtānu of the left	50
nāgir ekalli	228
rab šāqê	148
masennu AMA MAN	20[23]
masennu MÍ.É.GAL	8
Governor of Assur	12
Governor of Calah	5
Governor of Nineveh	4
lú*šaknūti*	14
PN lú*šaknu*	4

[19] Cf. above, p. 86, n. 41.

[20] Postgate *Taxation*: 11 and F.M. Fales, "Notes on Some Nineveh Horse Lists," *Assur* 1/3 (1974): 17ff.

[21] Postgate, *Taxation*: 11 and 18.

[22] Postgate, *Taxation*: 15-16.

[23] Note that there is a mistake in Postgate's list on page 15: he leaves out *ABL* 63 (= *SAA* XIII, 101) and so his total for the queen mother is four less than it should be.

It is clear that with the exception of the four top officials who were obviously acting in their roles as provincial governors, the queen mother is the individual who gives the most. It may be significant that she gives more horses than any of the governors of cities and more than twice as many as the queen herself. Without knowing whether we have all the horse texts that belong in this archive (highly unlikely)[24] or even whether they all date to the same year (probable), we cannot really grasp their full meaning. However, they do suggest that the queen mother was extremely wealthy, perhaps even wealthier than the queen. The fact that the queen mother delivered the horses in three different installments probably indicates that they came from three different estates, but this is not certain.

Members of the royal family as well as high-ranking palace officials were required to supply temples with daily offering needs and for special occasions,[25] but just what the tax situation was for these people remains unclear. We have evidence that Naqia made such payments to temples. *ABL* 368 and 569, letters to the queen mother from Nergal-šarrani, deal with temple offerings including oil, honey, aromatic plants, sheep, birds and cattle. These may have been daily offerings.[26] Whether these contributions, like the horses, can be regarded as a sort of tax, or whether they sometimes represent extra gifts, we cannot determine at this time. In fact neither letter explicitly states that the queen mother is providing the offerings and it is possible that she was not always expected to supply offerings from her own stock. The context remains obscure and we should be cautious about drawing conclusions from it. It is probable that as queen mother Naqia became responsible for supplying certain temples, as indeed, it appears each member of the royal family and some high officials were required to do.[27] Beyond that, we can say little about the tax structure for the Assyrian aristocracy.[28]

---

[24] There are other horse reports for which see Fales *Assur* 1/3, and Fales and Postgate, *SAA* XI, 107-122.

[25] Kataja and Whiting, *SAA* XII, 69, 77, and 80 are royal decrees specifying contributions to be made to temples by various officials; see also below, n. 27.

[26] Parpola, *LAS* 2: 300. Compare for example the lists of items appearing in *SAA* XIII, 76 and 77 to the list in *SAA* X, 350. See above, Chapter III, p, 45, for further discussion.

[27] See Fales and Postgate, *SAA* VII, part 14, "Miscellaneous Temple Offerings" 158-181; and part 15, "Offerings for the Aššur Temple " 182-219.

[28] For general information see Postgate, *Taxation*.

BIBLIOGRAPHY

Abusch, T. "Mesopotamian anti-witchcraft literature: Texts and Studies I." *JNES* 33 (1974) 259ff.

Ahmed, S. "Ashurbanipal and Šamaš-šum-ukin during Esarhaddon's Reign." *Abr-Naharain* 6 (1965-66) 53-62.

———. "Causes of Šamaš-šum-ukin's Uprising, 652-648 B.C." *Zeitschrift für alttestamentliche Wissenschaft* 79 (1967) 1-13.

———. *Simiramis.* Asamiyah, Baghdad: Dar al-Shuun al-Thaqafiyal al-Amnah, 1989.

———. *Southern Mesopotamia in the time of Ashurbanipal.* The Hague. Paris: Mouton, 1968.

Andrae, W. *Die Stelenreihen in Assur.* WVDOG 24. Leipzig, 1913.

Aro, J. "Remarks on the Practice of Extispicy in the time of Esarhaddon and Ashurbanipal." In *La divination en Mésopotamie ancienne et dans les régiones voisines.* Paris: Presses Universitaires de France, 1966. 109-17.

Arzt, J. "Neo-Assyrian Royal Women." *Yale Graduate Journal of Anthropology* 5 (1993) 45-56.

Banks, E.J. "Eight Oracular Responses to Esarhaddon." *AJSL* 14 (1897-98) 267-77.

Basmachi, F. "Miscellanea in the Iraq Museum." *Sumer* 18 (1962) 48-50.

Becking, Bob. *The Fall of Samaria: A Historical and Archaeological Study.* Studies in the History of the Ancient Near East 2. Leiden: E.J. Brill, 1992.

Behrens, E. *Assyrisch-babylonische Briefe kultischen Inhalts.* LSS 2/2. Leipzig, 1906.

Ben-Barak, Z. "The Queen Consort and the Struggle for Succession to the Throne." *CRRAI* 33 (1986) 33-40.

Biggs, R.D. "Medicine in Ancient Mesopotamia." *History of Science* 8 (1969) 94ff.

Boncquet, J. "De Koningin-moeder in de Neo-Assyrische periode." In A. Théodorides, P. Naster, and J. Ries (eds.), *Archéologie et philologie dans l'étude des civilisations orientales.* AOB 4 Leuven, 1986. 183-94.

Borger, R. *Die Inschriften Asarhaddons Königs von Assyrien.* AfO Beiheft 9. Graz, 1956.

———. "König Sanheribs Eheglück." *ARRIM* 6 (1988) 5-11.

———. Rev. of *Brief des Bischofs von Esagila an König Asarhaddon* by B. Landsberger. *BiOr* 29 (1972) 33-37.

Börker-Klähn, J. *Altvorderasiatische Bildstelen und vergleichbare Felsreliefs.* Baghdader Forschungen 4. Mainz, 1982.

Bottéro, J. "La Femme dans l'asie occidentale ancienne: Mesopotamie et Israel." In P. Grumal (ed.) *Histoire Mondiale de la Femme*, vol. 1. Paris: Nouvelle Librairie de France, 1965. 155-223.

Braun-Holzinger, E.A. *Figürliche Bronzen aus Mesopotamien.* Munich, 1984.

Brinkman, J.A. "Babylonia under the Assyrian Empire, 745-627." In *Power and Propaganda: A Symposium on Ancient Empires*, ed. M.T. Larsen. Mesopotamia 7. Copenhagen: Akedemisk Forlag, 1979. 223-50.

———. "The Elamite-Babylonian frontier in the Neo-Elamite period, 750-625 B.C." In *Fragmenta historiae elamicae: mélanges offerts à M.- J. Stève*, ed. L. De Meyer et al. Paris, 1986. 199-207.

———. "Foreign relations of Babylonia from 1600-625 B.C.: the Documentary Evidence," *AJA* 76 (1972) 271-81.

———. "Notes on Aramaeans and Chaldaeans in Southern Babylonia in the Early Seventh Century B.C." *OrNS* 46 (1977) 304-25.

———. *A Political History of Post-Kassite Babylonia.* Analecta Orientalia 43. Rome, 1968.

———. *Prelude to Empire: Babylonian Society and Politics, 747-626 B.C.*. Occasional Publications of the Babylonian Fund, 7. Philadelphia: The University Museum, 1984.

———. "Sennacherib's Babylonian Problem: An Interpretation" *JCS* 25 (1973) 89-95.

———. "Through a Glass Darkly: Esarhaddon's Retrospects on the Downfall of Babylon" *JAOS* 103 (1983) 35-42.

Brinkman, J.A. and D.A. Kennedy. "Documentary Evidence for the Economic Base of Early Neo-Babylonian Society: A Survey of Dated Babylonian Economic Texts, 721-626 B.C." *JCS* 35 (1983) 1-90.

Caplice, R. "Namburbi texts in the British Museum," *OrNS* 34 (1965) 105ff; 36 (1967) 1ff; 39 (1970) 111ff; 40 (1971) 133ff; 42 (1973) 508ff.

———. *The Akkadian Namburbi texts: An introduction.* SANE 1/1. Malibu, 1974.

Cogan, M. "Omens and Ideology in the Babylonian Inscriptions of Esarhaddon." In *History, Historiography and Interpretation*, ed. H. Tadmor and M. Weinfeld. Jerusalem: Magnes, 1986. 76-87.

———. "A Plaidoyer on behalf of the Royal Scribes." In *Ah, Assyria... Studies in Assyrian History and Ancient Near Eastern Historiography Presented to Hayim Tadmor*, ed. M. Cogan and I. Ephʿal. Scripta Hierosolymitana 33. Jerusalem: Magnes, 1991. 121-28.

Cole, S. and P. Machinist. *Letters from Priests to the Kings Esarhaddon and Ashurbanipal.* SAA XIII. Helsinki: Helsinki University Press, 1998.

Curtis, J. "Assyria as a Bronzeworking Centre in the Late Assyrian Period." In *Bronzeworking Centres of Western Asia c. 1000-539 B.C.*, ed. J. Curtis. London and New York, 1988. pp. 83-96 and plates 74-89.

Dellatre, A. "The Oracles Given in Favour of Esarhaddon." *The Babylonian and Oriental Record*, III, no. 2 (1889) 25-31.

Deller, K. "Die Briefe des Adad-šumu-uṣur." In lišān mitḫurti: *Festschrift Wolfram Freiherr von Soden zum 19.VI.1968 gewidmet von Schülern und Mitarbeitern*, ed. W. Röllig. AOAT 1. Kevalaer and Neukirchen-Vluyn, 1969.

———. "Zweisilbige Lautwerte des Typs KVKV in Neuassyrischen." *OrNS* 31 (1962) 7-26.

Dietrich, M. *Die Aramäer Südbabyloniens in der Sargonidenzeit (700-648)*. AOAT 7. Neukirchen-Vluyn, 1970.

———. "Neue Quellen zur Geschichte Babyloniens (I) (Ein Vorbericht)." *WO* 4 (1967-8) 61-103.

———. "Neue Quellen zur Geschichte Babyloniens (II) (Ein Vorbericht)." *WO* 4 (1967-8) 183-251.

———. "Neue Quellen zur Geschichte Babyloniens (II - Indizes)." *WO* 5 (1969-70) 51-56.

———. "Neue Quellen zur Geschichte Babyloniens (III): Die Briefe des Truppenkommandanten ^{d}Bēl-ibni aus dem Meerland (Ein Vorbericht)." *WO* 5 (1969-70) 176-90.

———. "Neue Quellen zur Geschichte Babyloniens (IV): Die Urkunden der Jahre 700 bis 651 aus dem Archiv des Urukäers Nabû-ušallim." *WO* 6 (1970-71) 157-62.

Donbaz, V. "Two Neo-Assyrian Stelae in the Antakya and Kahramanmaraş Museums." *ARRIM* 8 (1990) 5-24.

Donner, H. "Art und Herkunft des Amtes der Königinmutter im AltenTestament." in *Festschrift Johannes Friedrich zum 65. Geburtstag am 27. August 1958 gewidmet*, ed. R. von Kienle, et al. Heidelberg: Carl Winter Universitätsverlag, 1959. 105-45.

Driel, G. van. *The Cult of Aššur*. Assen, The Netherlands: Van Gorcum, 1969.

Fadhil, A. "Die in Nimrud/Kalḫu aufgefundene Grabinschrift der Jabâ." *BaM* 21 (1990) 461-70.

Fales, F.M. "Esarhaddon e il potere della divinazzazione." *Sopranaturale e potere nel mondo antico e nelle società tradizionali*. Eds. F.M. Fales and C. Grottanelli. Milan, 1985. 95-118.

———. "L'Ideologo Adad-šumu-uṣur." *Rendiconti dell' Accademia Nazionale dei Lincei*, 29 (1975) 453-96.

———. "A List of Assyrian and West Semitic Women's Names." *Iraq* 41 (1979) 55-73.

———. "New Assyrian Letters in the Kuyunjik Collection." *AfO* 27 (1980) 136-53.

———. "Notes on Some Nineveh Horse Lists." *Assur* 1/3 (1974) 5-24.

———. "On Aramaic Onomastics in the Neo-Assyrian Period." *Oriens Antiquus* 16 (1977) 41-68.

Fales, F.M. and J.N. Postgate. *Imperial Administrative Records, Part I: Palace and Temple Administration.* SAA VII. Helsinki: Helsinki University Press, 1992.

Falkner, M. "Die Eponymen der spätassyrische Zeit." *AfO* 17 (1954-56) 100-20.

Finkel, I.L. "A Report on Extispicies Performed for Sennacherib on Account of his Son Aššur-nadin-šumi." *SAAB* 1 (1987) 53.

Frahm, E. *Einleitung in die Sanherib-Inschriften.* AfO Beiheft 26. Wien, 1997.

Frame, G. *Babylonia 689-627 B.C.: A Political History.* Istanbul: Nederlands Historisch-Archaeologisch Instituut, 1992.

Frymer-Kensky, T. "The Tribulations of Marduk: the so-called 'Marduk Ordeal Text.'" *JAOS* 103 (1983) 131-41.

Galter, H.D. "Die Bautätigkeit Sanheribs am Aššurtempel." *OrNS* 53 (1984) 433-41.

———. "On Beads and Curses." *ARRIM* 5 (1987) 11-30.

Galter, H.D., L.D. Levine, and J.E. Reade. "The Colossi of Sennacherib's Palace and their Inscriptions." *ARRIM* 4 (1986) 32.

Garelli, P. "La propagande royale assyrienne." *Akkadica* 27 (1982) 16-29.

George, A. "Royal Tombs at Nimrud." *Minerva* I/1 (1990) 29-31.

Grayson, A.K. *Assyrian and Babylonian Chronicles.* TCS 5. Locust Valley, New York: J.J. Augustin, 1975.

———. "Assyrian Royal Inscriptions: Literary Characteristics." In *Assyrian Royal Inscriptions: New Horizons in Literary, Ideological, and Historical Analysis*, ed. F.M. Fales. Rome: Istituto per l'Oriente, 1981. 35-48.

———. *CAH* III/2. Chapters 23 and 24. Cambridge: Cambridge University Press, 1991. 103-61.

———. "Histories and Historians of the Ancient Near East: Assyria and Babylonia." *OrNS* 49 (1980) 140-94.

———. Letter to Dr. Basmachi. *Sumer* 19 (1963) 111-12.

Hallo, W.W. "Royal Inscriptions of Ur: a Typology." *Hebrew Union College Annual* 33 (1962) 1-43.

———. "From Qarqar to Carchemish: Assyria and Israel in the Light of New Discoveries." *Biblical Archaeologist* 23 (1960) 34-61 and 132.

———. *Origins: The Ancient Near Eastern Background of Some Modern Western Institutions.* Leiden: E.J. Brill, 1996.

Harrak, A. "The Royal Tombs of Nimrud and Their Jewelry." *CMS Bulletin* 20 (1990) 5-14.

Harper, R.F. *Assyrian and Babylonian Letters Belonging to the Kuyunjik Collection of the British Museum.* 14 vols. London and Chicago: University of Chicago. 1892-1914.

Heidel, A. and A.L. Oppenheim. "A New Hexagonal Prism of Esarhaddon (676 B.C.)." *Sumer* 12 (1956) 9-37 and pls. 1-12.

Herbordt, S. *Neuassyrische Glyptik des 8.-7. Jh. v. Ch.: unter besonderer Berücksichtigung der Siegelungen auf Tafeln und Tonverschlüssen.* SAAS 1. Helsinki: The Neo-Assyrian Text Corpus Project, 1992.

Hunger, H. *Astrological Reports to Assyrian Kings.* SAA VIII. Helsinki: Helsinki University Press, 1992.

Jacobsen, T. *Treasures of Darkness: A History of Mesopotamian Religion.* New Haven and London: Yale University Press, 1976.

Johns, C.H.W. *Assyrian Deeds and Documents Recording the Transfer of Property, Including the So-Called Private Contracts, Legal Decisions and Proclamations, Preserved in the Kouyunjik Collections of the British Museum, Chiefly of the 7th Century B.C.* 4 volumes. Cambridge: 1898, 1901, 1901, and 1923.

———. *An Assyrian Doomsday Book or Liber Censualis of the District round Harran in the Seventh Century B.C.* Assyriologische Bibliothek 17. Leipzig, 1901.

Kataja, L. and R. Whiting. *Grants, Decrees and Gifts of the Neo-Assyrian Period.* SAA XII. Helsinki: Helsinki University Press, 1995.

King, L.A. *Babylonian Boundary-Stones and Memorial-Tablets in the British Museum.* London, 1912.

Kinnier Wilson, J.V. *The Nimrud Wine Lists: A study of men and administration at the Assyrian capital in the 8th century B.C.* British School of Archaeology in Iraq, 1972.

———. "An Introduction to Babylonian Psychiatry." In *Studies in Honor of Benno Landsberger on his Seventy-fifth Birthday April 21, 1965*, ed. H.G. Güterbock and Th. Jacobsen. Assyriological Studies 16. Chicago, 1965. 289-98.

Klauber, E.G. *Politisch-religiöse Texte aus der Sargonidenzeit.* Leipzig: Eduard Pfeiffer, 1913.

Knudsen, E.E. "Fragments of Historical Texts from Nimrud II." *Iraq* 29 (1967) 48-49 and pls. 14-29.

Knudtzon, J.A. *Assyrische Gebete an den Sonnengott für Staat und königliches Haus aus der Zeit Asarhaddons und Asurbanipals.* 2 volumes. Leipzig: Eduard Pfeiffer, 1893.

Kohler, J. and A. Ungnad. *Assyrische Rechtsurkunden.* Leipzig: Eduard Pfeiffer, 1913.

Kudlek, M. and E. Mickler. *Solar and Lunar Eclipses of the Ancient Near East from 3000 B.C. to 0 with Maps.* AOATS 1. Neukirchen-Vluyn: Kevelaer and Neukirchener, 1971.

Kuhrt, A. *The Ancient Near East c. 3000 - 330 BC.* Two volumes. London and New York: Routledge, 1995.

Kwasman, T. *Neo-Assyrian Legal Documents in the Kouyunjik Collection of the British Museum.* Studia Pohl, Series Maior 14. Rome, 1988.

Kwasman, T. and S. Parpola. *Legal Transactions of the Royal Court of Nineveh, Part I.* SAA VI. Helsinki: Helsinki University Press, 1991.

Labat, R. "Asarhaddon et la ville de Zaqqap." *RA* 53 (1959) 113-18.

———. "Das Assyrische Reich unter den Sargoniden." *Fischer Welgeschichte (Band 4), Die Altorientalische Reiche, III: Die Erste Halfte des 1. Jahrtausends.* Edited by E. Cassin, J. Bottéro and J. Vercoutter. Frankfurt am Main: Fischer Bucherei, 1967. 68-93.

———. *Le caractère religieux de la royauté assyro-babylonienne.* Paris, 1939.

———. *Traité akkadien de diagnostics et pronostics médicaux.* Leiden, 1951.

Lambert, W.G. "An Eye-stone of Esarhaddon's Queen and Other Similar Gems." *RA* 63 (1969) 65-71.

Landsberger, B. *Brief des Bischofs von Esagila an König Asarhaddon.* Mededelingen der Koninklijke Nederlandse Akademie van Wetenschappen, Afd. Letterkunde, Nieuve Reeks, Deel 28, No. 6. Amsterdam: Noord-Hollanische Vitgeurs Maatschappij, 1965.

Landsberger, B. and Th. Bauer. "Zu neuveröffentlichen Geschichtsquellen der Zeit von Asarhaddon bis Nabonid." *ZA* 37 (1927) 61-98.

Lanfranchi, G.B. "Scholars and Scholarly Tradition in Neo-Assyrian Times: A Case Study" *SAAB* 3 (1989) 99-114.

Lanfranchi, G.B. and S. Parpola. *The Correspondence of Sargon II, Part II.* SAA V. Helsinki: Helsinki Univeristy Press, 1990.

Langdon, S. *Tammuz and Ishtar: A Monograph upon Babylonian Religion and Theology Containing Extensive Extracts from the Tammuz Liturgies and All of the Arbela Oracles.* Oxford: Oxford University Press, 1914.

Larsen, M.T. "Unusual Eponymy-Datings from Mari and Assyria." *RA* 68 (1974) 15-24.

Leichty, E. "Esarhaddon, King of Assyria." In *Civilizations of the Ancient Near East*, volume II. ed. J. Sasson et al. New York: Scribner, 1995. 949-58.

Leichty, E. "Esarhaddon's 'Letter to the Gods.'" In *Ah, Assyria... Studies in Assyrian History and Ancient Near Eastern Historiography Presented to Hayim Tadmor,* ed. M. Cogan and I. Eph'al. Scripta Hierosolymitana 33. Jerusalem, 1991. 52-57.

Levine, L.D. "Manuscripts, Texts and the Study of the Neo-Assyrian Royal Inscriptions." In *Assyrian Royal Inscriptions: New Horizons in Literary, Ideological, and Historical Analysis*, ed. F.M. Fales. Rome: Istituto per l'Oriente, 1981. 49-70.

Lewy, H. "Nitokris-Naqî'a." *JNES* 11 (1952) 264-86.

Liverani, M. "The Ideology of the Assyrian Empire." In *Power and Propaganda: a Symposium on Ancient Empires*, ed. M.T. Larsen. Mesopotamia 7. Copenhagen, 1979. 297-318.

Livingstone, A. *Court Poetry and Literary Miscellanea.* SAA III. Helsinki: Helsinki University Press, 1989.

Luckenbill, D.D. *Ancient Records of Assyria and Babylonia.* 2 volumes. Chicago: University of Chicago Press, 1926 and 1927.

———. *Annals of Sennacherib.* Oriental Institute Publications 2. Chicago: University of Chicago Press, 1924.

Machinist, P. Review of *Death in Mesopotamia: Papers Read at the XXVIe Rencontre Assyriologique Internationale.* Edited by B. Alster. *JAOS* 104 (1980) 568-70.

Mallowan, M.E.L. *Nimrud and its Remains.* 2 volumes. New York: Dodd, Mead and Co., 1966.

———. "The Excavations at Nimrud (Kalḫu) 1955." *Iraq* 18 (1956) 1-21.

Matsushima, E. "Le rituel hiérogamique de Nabû." *Acta Sumerologica* 9 (1987) 131-75.

Meier, G. *Die assyrische Beschwörgungsammlung Maqlû.* AfO Beiheft 2. Berlin, 1937.

Meissner, B. "Naki'a." *MDVAG* 8/3 (1903) 96-101.

Menzel, B. *Assyrische Tempel.* 2 volumes. Studia Pohl, Series Maior 10. Rome: Biblical Institute Press, 1981.

Menzel-Wortmann, B. "Der ^LÚ^GAL *danibata* in neuassyrischer Zeit." *Mesopotamia* 21 (1986) 213-27.

Messerschmidt, L. *Keilschrifttexte aus Assur historischen Inhalts I.* WVDOG 16. Leipzig, 1911.

Millard, A.R. "Assyrians and Arameans." *Iraq* 45 (1983) 101-108.

———. *Eponyms of the Assyrian Empire, 910-612 BC.* SAAS 2. Helsinki: The Neo-Assyrian Text Corpus Project, 1994.

Nissinen, M. *References to Prophecy in Neo-Assyrian Sources.* SAAS 7. Helsinki: The Neo-Assyrian Text Corpus Project, 1998.

Oates, D. "Ezida: The Temple of Nabu." *Iraq* 19 (1957) 26-39 and pl. 12.

Olmstead, A.T.E. *History of Assyria.* Chicago: University of Chicago Press, 1923.

Oppenheim, A.L. "Assyriological Gleanings IV." *BASOR* 107 (1947) 7-11.

———. "Divination and Celestial Observation in the Last Assyrian Empire." *Centaurus* 14 (1969) 97-135.

———. "Idiomatic Akkadian." *JAOS* 61 (1941) 251-

———. *Letters from Mesopotamia.* Chicago: University of Chicago Press, 1967.

Oppenheim, A.L. "Neo-Assyrian and Neo-Babylonian Empires." In *Propaganda and Communication in World History I: The Symbolic Instrument in Early Times*, ed. A.L. Oppenheim, H.D. Lasswell, D. Lerner and H. Speiser. Honolulu: University Press of Hawaii, 1979. 111-44.

———. "Notes on the Harper Letters." *JAOS* 64 (1944) 190-96.

Parpola, S. "Assyrian Library Records." *JNES* 42 (1983) 1-29.

———. *Assyrian Prophecies*. SAA IX. Helsinki: Helsinki University Press, 1997.

———. "Assyrian Royal Inscriptions and Neo-Assyrian Letters." In *Assyrian Royal Inscriptions: New Horizons in Literary, Ideological, and Historical Analysis*, ed. F.M. Fales. Rome: Istituto per l'Oriente, 1981. 117-41.

———. "Collations to Neo-Assyrian Legal Texts from Nineveh." *Assur* 2/5 (1979) 1-89.

———. *The Correspondence of Sargon II, Part I*. SAA I. Helsinki: Helsinki University Press, 1987.

———. "The Forlorn Scholar." In *Language, Literature and History: Philological and Historical Studies presented to Erica Reiner*, ed. F. Rochberg-Halton. AOS, 1987. 257-78.

———. "A Letter from Šamaš-šum-ukin to Esarhaddon." *Iraq* 34 (1972) 21-34.

———. *Letters from Assyrian and Babylonian Scholars*. SAA X. Helsinki: Helsinki University Press, 1993.

———. *Letters from Assyrian Scholars to the Kings Esarhaddon and Assurbanipal*. AOAT 5/1-2. Kevelaer and Neukirchen-Vluyn, 1970 and 1983.

———. *Letters from Assyrian Scholars to the Kings Esarhaddon and Ashurbanipal, part II A: Introduction and Appendices*. Diss., University of Helsinki. Neukirchen-Vluyn, 1971.

———. "The Murderer of Sennacherib." In *Death in Mesopotamia: Papers Read at the XXVIe Rencontre Assyriologique Internationale*, ed. B. Alster. Mesopotamia 8. Copenhagen, 1980.

———. *Neo-Assyrian Letters from the Kuyunjik Collection*. CT 53. London: The British Museum, 1979.

———. *Neo-Assyrian Toponyms*. AOAT 6. Kevalaer and Neukirchen-Vluyn, 1970.

———. "Neo-Assyrian Treaties from the Royal Archives of Nineveh." *JCS* 39 (1987) 161-189.

———. "The Neo-Assyrian Word for 'Queen.'" *SAAB* 2 (1988) 73-76.

———. Rev. of *Taxation and Conscription in the Assyrian Empire*. By J.N. Postgate. *ZA* 65 (1975) 293-296.

Parpola, S. and K. Watanabe. *Neo-Assyrian Treaties and Loyalty Oaths*. SAA II. Helsinki: Helsinki University Press, 1988.

Parpola, S. and R.M. Whiting (eds.). *Assyria 1995. Proceedings of the 10th Anniversary Symposium of the Neo-Assyrian Text Corpus Project, Helsinki, September 7-11, 1995*. Helsinki: The Neo-Assyrian Text Corpus Project, 1997.

Parrot, A. and J. Nougayrol. "Asarhaddon et Naqi'a sur un Bronze du Louvre (AO 20.185)." *Syria* 33 (1956) 147-60.

Pettinato, G. *Semiramis: Herrin über Assur und Babylon*. Munich and Zürich: Artemis, 1988.

Pfeiffer, R.H. *State Letters of Assyria: A Transliteration and Translation of 355 Official Assyrian Letters Dating from the Sargonid Period (722-625 B.C.)*. AOS 6. New Haven, 1935.

Porter, B.N. *Images, Power and Politics: Figurative Aspects of Esarhaddon's Babylonian Policy*. Memoirs of the American Philosophical Society, volume 208. Philadelphia: American Philosophical Society, 1993.

———. "Symbols of Power: Figurative Aspects of Esarhaddon's Babylonian Policy (681-669)." Ph.D. dissertation, University of Pennsylvania, 1987.

Postgate, J.N. "The bit akiti in Assyrian Nabu Temples." *Sumer* 30 (1974) 51-74.

———. *Fifty Neo-Assyrian Legal Documents.* Warminster: Aris and Philips, 1976.

———. *Neo-Assyrian Royal Grants and Decrees.* Studia Pohl, Series Maior 1. Rome, 1969.

———. Rev. of *Neo-Assyrian Legal Documents.* Studia Pohl, Series Maior 14. By T. Kwasman. *OrNS* 60 (1991) 123-24.

———. Rev. of *Assyrische Tempel.* Studia Pohl, Series Maior 10. By B. Menzel. *Journal of Semitic Studies* 18 (1983) 155-59.

———. *Taxation and Conscription in the Assyrian Empire.* Studia Pohl, Series Maior 3. Rome, 1974.

Rawlinson, H.C. *The Cuneiform Inscriptions of Western Asia, Volume IV: A Selection from the Miscellaneous Inscriptions of Assyria.* London: R.E. Bowler, 1875.

Reade, J.E. "Ideology and Propaganda in Assyrian Art." In *Power and Propaganda: a Symposium on Ancient Empires*, ed. M.T. Larsen. Mesopotamia 7. Copenhagen, 1979. 329-44.

———. "Was Sennacherib a Feminist?" *CRRAI* 33 (1986) 139-45.

Reiner, E. *Šurpu. A Collection of Sumerian and Akkadian Incantations.* AfO Beiheft 11. Graz, 1958

Roth, M.T. Review of *Letters to Assyrian Scholars.* By S. Parpola. *ZA* 75 (1985) 307-309.

Russell, J.M. *Sennacherib's Palace Withut Rival at Nineveh.* Chicago and London: University of Chicago Press, 1991.

Sachs, A.J. "The Late Assyrian Royal Seal Type." *Iraq* 15 (1953) 167-70.

Scheil, V. "Notes d'épigraphie et d'archéologie assyriennes." *Recueil de travaux relatifs à la philologie et à l'archéologie égyptiennes et assyriennes* 20 (1988) 200-210.

Schmidtke, F. *Asarhaddons Statthalterschaft in Babylonien und seine Thronbesteigung in Assyrien 681 v. Chr.* AOTU 1/2. Leiden, 1916.

Schramm, W. "War Semiramis assyrische Regentin?" *Historia* 21 (1972) 513ff.

Smith, S.A. "Assyrian Letters, II." *Proceedings of the Society of Biblical Archaeology* 10 (1887-88) 60-72.

———. "Assyrian Letters, IV." *Proceedings of the Society of Biblical Archaeology* 10 (1887-88) 305-15.

Soden, W. von. *Herrscher im Alten Orient.* Berlin, 1954.

———. "Gibt es ein Zeugnis dafür, daß die Babylonier an die Wiederauferstehung Marduks geglaubt haben?" *ZA* 51 (1954) 130-66.

———. "Ein neues Bruchstück des assyrischen Komentars zum Mardukordal." *ZA* 52 (1955) 224-34.

Streck, M. *Assurbanipal und die letzten assyrischen König bis zum Untergang Niniveh's.* VAB 7. Leipzig: J.C. Hinrichs, 1916.

Tadmor, H. "Autobiographical Apology in the Royal Assyrian Literature." In *History, Historiography and Interpretation: Studies in biblical and cuneiform literatures*, ed. H. Tadmor and M. Weinfeld. Jerusalem: Magnes Press, 1984. 36-57.

Tadmor, H. "History and Ideology in the Assyrian Royal Inscriptions." In *Assyrian Royal Inscriptions: New Horizons in Literary, Ideological and Historical Analysis*, ed. F.M. Fales. Rome, Istituto per l'Oriente, 1981. 13-34.

———. "The 'Sin of Sargon.'" *Eretz Israel* 5 (1958) 93* (English Summary) and 150-63 (in Hebrew).

Tadmor, H., B. Landsberger, and S. Parpola. "The Sin of Sargon and Sennacherib's Last Will." *SAAB* 3 (1989) 3-51.

Turner, G. "Tell Nebi Yūnus: The *ekal māšarti* of Nineveh." *Iraq* 32 (1970) 68-85.

Ungnad, A. "Eponymen." *RLA* 2. 412-57.

Van De Mieroop, M. "An Inscribed Bead of Queen Zakûtu." In *The Tablet and the Scroll: Near Eastern Studies in Honor of William W. Hallo*, ed. M. Cohen, D.C. Snell and D.B. Weisberg. CDL Press, 1993. 259-61.

Watanabe, K. *Die* adê-*Vereidigung anlässlich der Thronfolgeregelung Asarhaddons.* BaM Beiheft 3. Berlin, 1987.

Waterman, L. *Royal Correspondence of the Assyrian Empire.* 4 volumes. Ann Arbor: University of Michigan, 1930.

———. "Some Koyunjik Letters and Related Texts." *AJSL* 29 (1912) 1-36.

Weidner, E.F. "Assurbanipal in Assur." *AfO* 13 (1939-40) 204-18.

———. "Hochverrat gegen Asarhaddon." *AfO* 17 (1954-6) 5-9.

Weinfeld, M. "Semiramis: Her Name and Her Origin." In *Ah, Assyria... Studies in Assyrian History and Ancient Near Eastern Historiography Presented to Hayim Tadmor*, ed. M. Cogan and I. Eph'al. Scripta Hierosolymitana 33. Jerusalem: Magnes, 1991. 99-103.

Weippert, M. "Assyrische Prophetien der Zeit Asarhaddons und Assurbanipals." In *Assyrian Royal Inscriptions: New Horizons in Literary, Ideological and Historical Analysis*, ed. F.M. Fales. Rome: Istituto per l'Oriente, 1981. 71-116.

Wiseman, D.J. "The Vassal-Treaties of Esarhaddon." *Iraq* 20 (1958) 1-100.

Winckler, H. *Altorientalische Forschungen*, II. Leipzig, 1898.

Winter, I. "The Program of the Throneroom of Assurnaṣirpal II." In *Essays on Near Eastern Art and Archaeology in Honor of Charles Kyrle Wilkinson*, ed. P. Harper and H. Pittman. New York: The Metropolitan Museum of Art, 1983. 15-32.

———. "Royal Rhetoric and the Development of Historical Narrative in Neo-Assyrian Reliefs." *Studies in Visual Communications* 7 (1981) 2-38.

Zadok, R. *On West Semites in Babylonia during the Chaldean and Achaemenian Periods: An Onomastic Study.* Jerusalem: H.J. and Z. Wanaarta and Tel-Aviv University, 1977.

INDEXES

Numbers in italics refer to footnote numbers to be found on the page number immediately preceding. Footnotes are not indexed unless the referenced term appears only in the footnote.

Personal Names

Abi-rami: 2, 15-16
Adad-nirari (III): 3
Adad-šumu-uṣur: 44 *66*, 75, 79 *2*, 81 *18*, 82, 84, 96-97
Adapa: 33, 75
Aḫat-abiša: 28, 102
Amuše: 77
Aplâ: 54-55, 95
Ashurbanipal: 1-4, 6-7, 9-10, 13 *1*, 14, 20 *48*, 23, 31, 32 *5*, 33 *15*, 34-36, 50-52, 57, 59-60, 63 *14*, 69, 72, 74-75, 81 *18*, 85-86, 88-90, 92, 97, 105 *1*, 111
Asqudu: 86 *41*
Ašaredu: 6, 67-70, 95
  panû: 68-69
  qatnu: 68-69
Aššur-etel-ilani: 35 *28*
Aššur-etellu-mukin-apli: 17 *28*
Aššur-ili-muballissu: 17
Aššur-nadin-šumi: 9, 13 *1*, 17-18, 20-22, 23 *63*, 91
Aššur-šumu-ušabši: 17
Atalia: 14

Bel-aḫḫešu: 109
Bel-remanni: 75-76
Bel-ušezib: 27, 96
Bir-yama: 109

Dadî: 75-76, 97
Dadâ: 27
Damqa: 45

Esarhaddon:
  accession of: 22-29
  as king: 31-32
  Babylonian policy of: 37-38, 59, 61-62
  health of: 35-36, 81
  promotion to crown prince: 16-17, 22-24
  rebellion against: 79-82
Ešarra-ḫamat: 9, 61-62

Gabbi: 109

Ḫamunaia: 77
Hezekiah: 14
Ḫumanigaš: 65
Ḫumban-ḫaltaš: 66

Iabaia: 14 *7*
Idu'a: 63
Iltadaya: 109

Inurta-ila'i: 109
Issar-na'id: 108
Issar-šumu-ereš: 33, 73-75, 81, 94, 98

Libbali-šarrat: 15 *18*, 50-51, 52 *89*, 72

Mar-Issar: 49, 54, 55 *98*, 70-71, 97
Marduk-apla-iddina (II): 34, 49, 63, 66
Marduk-šakin-šumi: 32, 75, 82, 96
Martu: 108
Mutakkil-Aššur: 109

Na'id-Marduk: 7, 63-67, 95
Nabû-bel-šumate: 64 *21*, 67 *30*
Nabû-duru-uṣur: 109
Nabû-eṭir: 64
Nabû-iqbi: 69 *38*
Nabû-iqiša: 55 *99*, 70 *46*
Nabû-le'i: 54
Nabû-nadin-šumi: 18 *33*, 44 *66*, 97, 106
Nabû-naṣir: 96
Nabû-reḫtu-uṣur: 110
Nabû-šarru-uṣur: 23, 109
Nabû-šumu-iškun: 24, 34 *21*, 44 *66*, 47 *77*
Nabû-šumu-lišir: 55-56, 58, 95
Nabû-ušallim: 66
Nabû-ušezib: 109
Nabû-zer-kitti-lišir: 34, 63, 64 *20*, 66 *25*
Nabû-zeru-iddina: 52, *90*
Nadinu: 98, 110
Naqia: see also Zakutu
  as Nitokris: 3
  as Zakutu: 14, 43-44
  building inscription of: 38-41
  consulting oracles: 27-28
  contributions to temples: 44-45, 52-53
  curse of: 33, 74-75
  dedications to deities: 43-44
  illness of: 82-85
  involvement in Babylonia: 53-58, 61-71
  on a bronze relief: 15, 25-26, 47-52
  origins of: 13-16
  position as queen: 19-23, 25-28
  position in Assyria: 71-77
  statue of: 46
  wisdom of: 32-33, 75
  Zakutu Treaty: 86-90
Nergal-ašarid: 68 *35*
Nergal-šarrani: 44, 47 *77*, 93, 112
Ningal-iddina: 65-66

Geographical Names

God and Temple Names

Texts Cited or Discussed

Texts are generally indexed only under the most recent edition.

State Archives of Assyria Studies

VOLUME I
Neuassyrische Glyptik des 8.-7. Jh. v. Chr.
unter besonderer Berücksichtigung der Siegelungen
auf Tafeln und Tonverschlüsse
by Suzanne Herbordt
1992

VOLUME II
The Eponyms of the Assyrian Empire 910–612 BC
by Alan Millard
1994

VOLUME III
The Use of Numbers and Quantifications
in the Assyrian Royal Inscriptions
by Marco De Odorico
1995

VOLUME IV
Nippur in Late Assyrian Times
c. 755–612 BC
by Steven W. Cole
1996

VOLUME V
Neo-Assyrian Judicial Procedures
by Remko Jas
1996

VOLUME VI
Die neuassyrischen Privatrechtsurkunden
als Quelle für Mensch und Umwelt
by Karen Radner
1997